Burnaby's Travels Through North America;

𝔖𝔬𝔲𝔯𝔠𝔢 𝔅𝔬𝔬𝔨𝔰 𝔬𝔣 𝔄𝔪𝔢𝔯𝔦𝔠𝔞𝔫 ℌ𝔦𝔰𝔱𝔬𝔯𝔶.

BURNABY TRAVELS.

SOURCE BOOKS OF AMERICAN HISTORY.

Edited with Notes and Introduction by
RUFUS ROCKWELL WILSON

Andrew Burnaby. Travels Through the Middle Settlements of North America, 1759-60.

Reprinted from the last (the third) edition of 1798.

Small 8vo, cloth, with map. $2.00 *net.*

William Heath. Memoirs of the American War.

Reprinted from edition of 1798.

Small 8vo, cloth. $2.50 *net.*

W. W. Canfield. Legends of the Iroquois.

Small 8vo, cloth, illustrated. $1.50 *net.*

IN PREPARATION:

William Moultrie. Memoirs of the American Revolution.

Freiin von Reidesel. Letters and Journal.

Thomas J. Dimsdale. Vigilantes of Montana.

AND OTHERS.

A. WESSELS COMPANY, NEW YORK.

BURNABY'S TRAVELS
THROUGH
NORTH AMERICA

*REPRINTED FROM THE THIRD
EDITION OF 1798*

WITH INTRODUCTION AND NOTES BY

RUFUS ROCKWELL WILSON

New York
A. WESSELS COMPANY
1904

The Plimpton Press Norwood Mass

CONTENTS.

EDITOR'S FOREWORD.

THE author of the volume to which this serves as introduction was born in 1734 at Asfordby, in Leicestershire, the eldest son and namesake of the Reverend Andrew Burnaby, a well-to-do clergyman of the Church of England, who served successively as vicar of St. Margaret's, Leicester, rector of Asfordby and prebendary of Lincoln.

The younger Burnaby was admitted into Westminster School in 1748, and proceeded thence to Queen's College, Cambridge, where he took the degree of Bachelor of Arts in 1754, and three years later, that of Master of Arts. In 1759 and 1760, he travelled through the American colonies, and from 1762 to 1767, having in the meantime taken orders, he was chaplain to the British factory at Leghorn. During his sojourn in Italy he explored all parts of that country and travelled in Corsica, of which, in 1804, he published an account. In 1769, soon after his return to England, he was nominated to the vicarage of Greenwich, and in 1786 he was pre-

sented to the archdeaconry of Leicester. He succeeded to large estates in Huntingdonshire on his
father's death in 1767, but Baggrave Hall, Leicestershire, the inheritance of his wife Anna, daughter of
John Edwyn, whom he married in 1770, was his
favorite place of residence. He died at Blackheath,
on March 9, 1812, and within a fortnight his wife
followed him to the grave. One of his descendants
in the fourth generation was Frederick Burnaby, the
soldier and traveller, who was killed in 1885 at the
battle of Abu Klea in the Soudan.

Burnaby tells in his introduction how the record
of his travels through the American colonies found
its way into print. First published in 1775, it
reached a second edition within a year and was
speedily translated into French and German. The
original was reissued in much enlarged form in 1798,
and from that edition the present reprint is made.
Burnaby's book well deserves a new lease of life, for
he was an acute though kindly observer, and his visit
to the colonies fell in an interesting and critical time:
the Seven Years' War which wrought the downfall
of the French power in America was just drawing to
a close, and in the political sky was heard the low,
insistent rumblings of the storm which was to break
at Concord and Bunker Hill.

It should be remembered that the author's point
of view was that of a devoted minister of the Church
of England and loyal supporter of the crown. Thus

Foreword

his religious and political inclinings color his impressions of country and people. There is evidence on every page, however, that he was moved by a sincere purpose to be truthful and just, and he helps not a little to a fuller and more accurate knowledge of a confused and troubled period in our history. The editor has conformed the author's spelling of proper names to present usages, and has added such notes as seemed necessary to make certain of his allusions clear to the average reader.

R. R. W.

TRAVELS

THROUGH THE

MIDDLE SETTLEMENTS

IN

NORTH AMERICA,

IN THE YEARS 1759 AND 1760;

WITH

OBSERVATIONS UPON THE STATE OF THE COLONIES

By the Rev. ANDREW BURNABY, D.D.
ARCHDEACON OF LEICESTER AND VICAR OF GREENWICH.

EDITION THE THIRD;

REVISED, CORRECTED, AND GREATLY ENLARGED, BY THE AUTHOR.

LONDON

PRINTED FOR T. PAYNE, AT THE MEWS-GATE.

1798

[*Facsimile Title Page, Third Edition.*]

TO

SIR JOHN DICK, Bart.

&c. &c. &c.

THIS THIRD EDITION OF

TRAVELS THROUGH THE MIDDLE SETTLEMENTS

IN NORTH AMERICA,

IS,

IN TESTIMONY OF THE SINCEREST AFFECTION AND GRATITUDE,

MOST RESPECTFULLY INSCRIBED,

BY HIS EVER FAITHFUL

AND OBLIGED HUMBLE SERVANT,

ANDREW BURNABY.

GREENWICH, August 27, 1798.

PREFACE

THIRD EDITION.

THE two former Editions of these Travels were published, one immediately after the other, at a moment, when events of the greatest magnitude, and importance to this country, were depending; and when the minds of men were extremely agitated and alarmed for the fate of the British Empire. A rupture between Great Britain and her American Colonies was seriously apprehended: and as men foresaw, or at least fancied they foresaw, very calamitous consequences arising from so disastrous an event, it was generally wished that the evil might, if possible, be prevented; and a reconciliation happily effected, before matters were carried to extremity. The Author, flattered by his friends, and perhaps a little also by vanity, presumed to hope, that the publication of his tour through the Middle Settlements in North America might, in some degree, conduce to this desirable end: and as the meas-

Preface

ures to be adopted by Government were at that time under the deliberation of Parliament, it was thought expedient to submit it to the Public, before any resolutions were formed that might eventually be decisive of the fate of the British Empire. There was not time, therefore, to publish the Work in so full and correct a manner, as the materials in the Author's possession would otherwise have enabled him to do. He confined himself to general, and what he judged leading, circumstances; and postponed the insertion of others to more favourable and tranquil times. The two former Editions, however, being now entirely out of print, he deems it expedient to publish a third Edition, revised, corrected, and greatly enlarged by the insertion of new matter; particularly by several statistical tables referring to the Commerce of America; and some authentic Memoirs of Thomas late Lord Fairfax, and of the several branches of that noble house now domiciliated in Virginia, both of which have been derived from the best and most unquestionable authority. — The Work for these reasons, and from its being almost the only account of the Middle Settlements, during the period of their happiest and most flourishing state, may possibly, notwithstanding the separation that has since taken place, be still interesting, at least to individuals: and the Author offers the present Edition to the Public, with the same assurance as he did the former ones; viz. that he believes the contents to be strictly and literally true. If, however, some slight errors may accidentally and undesignedly have been committed, and any one will have the goodness to point them out, the Author will think himself highly obliged by the information, and will avail himself of the first opportunity to acknowledge and correct them.

The astonishing events that have taken place since the publication of the two former Editions, will probably expose the Author's opinion concerning the termination and final issue of the American contest to animadversion: but in vindication of himself, he must be permitted to observe, —

That it was not within the sphere of calculation to suppose,

1st. That the British ministry would persist in requiring unconditional submission from the colonies, till it was too late to recede; and the opportunity was lost, and for ever gone by:

2dly. That when coercive measures had been resolved upon, they would have been enforced in so ruinous and so ineffectual a manner:

3dly That, during the war, any member in opposition would have declared publicly, that he corresponded with, and wished success to, the Americans, then in arms against the king:

Still less was it within the sphere of calculation to suppose,

That France, though it might be expected that

she would so far interfere in the contest as to endeavour to distress and embarrass this country,
would send troops to America, to the irreparable
ruin of her own finances, in order to make the Americans free and independent states:

Least of all was it within the sphere of calculation
to suppose,

That Spain would join in a plan inevitably leading, though by slow and imperceptible steps, to the
final loss of all her rich possessions in South America.

There were indeed enlightened minds both in
France and in Spain, who foresaw what has since
happened, and who deprecated any interference in the
dispute, and recommended the observance of a strict
neutrality: And the unfortunate Lewis the sixteenth
himself is said to have shewn the greatest repug-
nance to the treaty with the Americans, and to have
declared in the bitterness of sorrow, when he signed
it, that he had signed the warrant for his own ruin
and destruction

In August, 1792, the Author was at Cologne; and
there accidentally falling in with the Duke of Bour-
bon, and several French noblemen of his suite, the
conversation naturally turned upon the situation and
affairs of France; and the author expressing his surprise at the impolicy of the French ministry in engaging so deeply in the American war, and deducing
from thence the present miseries of France, one of
the courtiers with great emotion exclaimed, — "Ah,

Preface

"monsieur, c'est bien vrai; nous avons mal calculé!"
— But the die is cast, and it is too late to moralize.

The reader will doubtless be surprised, when the Author declares, that he has not altered his sentiments since the year 1775, in regard to the American war and its consequences. He still thinks, that the separation might, in the first instance, have been prevented: that coercive measures, when resolved upon, might have been enforced, comparatively speaking, without bloodshed; and with great probability of success: that the present union of the American States will not be permanent or last for any considerable length of time: that that extensive country must necessarily be divided into separate states and kingdoms: and that America will never, at least for many ages, become formidable to Europe; or acquire, what has been so frequently predicted, universal empire. The Author thinks he could assign plausible reasons at least for these various opinions; but it is better that they should be consigned to oblivion. The wise Disposer of events has decreed, that America shall be independent of Great Britain; that she is so, may ultimately perhaps be advantageous to both countries; at least it will be owing to excess of folly if it be highly disadvantageous to either. Let us supplicate Heaven to unite them in permanent friendship and affection; and to preserve inviolate that alliance, that harmony and connection, which religion, moral habits, lan-

guage, interest, origin, and innumerable other considerations, can never cease to point out and recommend to them.

INTRODUCTION.

A FEW days before I embarked for America, being in a coffee-house with some friends, and discoursing of things relative to that country, an elderly gentleman advancing towards the box where we were sitting, addressed himself to me in the following manner: "Sir," said he, "you "are young, and just entering into the world; I am "old, and upon the point of leaving it: allow me "therefore to give you one piece of advice, which is "the result of experience; and which may possibly, "some time or other, be of use to you. You are "going to a country where every thing will appear "new and wonderful to you; but it will appear so "only for a while; for the novelty of it will daily wear "off; and in time it will grow quite familiar to you. "Let me, therefore, recommend to you to note in "your pocket-book every circumstance that may "make an impression upon you; for be assured, sir, "though it may afterward appear familiar and un- "interesting to yourself, it will not appear so to your

Introduction

"friends, who have never visited that country, for "they will be entertained by it."

The following observations were the result of this advice; they were written upon the several spots to which they refer; and were intended for no other purpose, than that of serving as memorandums. They appeared, by the time I returned to Europe, according to the gentleman's prediction, so very familiar to me, that I scarcely thought them deserving of the perusal of my friends. Some of these, however, were so obliging as to bestow upon them that trouble; and it is by their advice, and the consideration of the present critical situation of affairs, that I now submit them to the judgment of the public. — Whatever may be their merit, which I fear is but small, I can assure the reader of one thing, I believe they are generally true. They are the fruit of the most impartial inquiries, and best intelligence, that I was able to procure in the different colonies which I visited. If I have been led into any error, or have misrepresented any thing, it has been undesignedly: a spirit of party is universally prevalent in America, and it is not always an easy matter to arrive at the knowledge of truth; but I believe, in general, I have been pretty successful. I conversed indiscriminately with persons of all parties; and endeavoured, by allowing for prejudices and collating their different accounts, to get at the true one. If I have any doubt myself about any particular part of

Introduction

the following observations (and it is one in which I wish I may be found to have been misinformed), it is that which relates to the character of the Rhode Islanders. I was exceedingly ill at that place, and had not the same opportunity of procuring information as elsewhere. I conversed with but few gentlemen, and they were principally of one party; but they were gentlemen of such universal good character, that I could not but rely in some measure on the accounts with which they favoured me. Some allowance, however, I did make for prejudice; and I am desirous that the reader should make a still larger one; indeed, I should be happy to stand corrected in regard to what I have said of that people, as no one can have less pleasure in speaking unfavourably of mankind than myself.

I have studiously avoided all technical or scientific terms; such to the informed reader are unnecessary, to the uninformed one they are unintelligible and perplexing: in relations of this kind they have always an appearance of affectation and pedantry.

For the most valuable part of the following collection, I mean the Diary* of the Weather, I am entirely indebted to my esteemed friend, Francis Fauquier, esq., son of the late worthy lieutenant-governor of Virginia, who very obligingly transmitted it to me from Williamsburg, while I resided, as chaplain to

* See Appendix, No. 1.

the British factory, at Leghorn; and has allowed me to make the use of it which I have here done.

The present unhappy differences subsisting amongst us, with regard to America, will, I am sensible, expose the publication of this account to much censure and criticism; but I can truly aver, that I have been led to it by no party motive whatsoever. My first attachment, as it is natural, is to my native country; my next is to America; and such is my affection for both, that I hope nothing will ever happen to dissolve that union, which is necessary to their common happiness. Let every Englishman and American, but for a moment or two, substitute themselves in each other's place, and, I think, a mode of reconciliation will soon take effect.—Every American will then perceive the reasonableness of acknowledging the supremacy of the British legislature; and every Englishman, perhaps, the hardship of being taxed where there is no representation, or assent.

There is scarcely any such thing, I believe, as a perfect government; and solecisms are to be found in all. The present disputes are seemingly the result of one.—Nothing can be more undeniable than the supremacy of Parliament over the most distant branches of the British Empire: for although the king being esteemed, in the eye of the law, the original proprietor of all the lands in the kingdom; all lands, upon defect of heirs to succeed to an inheritance, escheat to the king; and all new discovered lands vest in him: yet in neither case can he exempt them from the jurisdiction of the legislature of the kingdom.

He may grant them, under leases or charters, to individuals or companies, with liberty of making rules and regulations for the internal government and improvement of them; but such regulations must ever be consistent with the laws of the kingdom, and subject to their control.

On the other hand, I am extremely dubious, whether it be consistent with the general principles of liberty (with those of the British constitution I think it is not) to tax where there is no representation: the arguments hitherto adduced from Manchester and Birmingham, and other great towns, not having representatives, are foreign to the subject; at least they are by no means equal to it;—for every inhabitant, possessed of forty shillings freehold, has a vote in the election of members for the county: but it is not the persons, but the property of men that is taxed, and there is not a foot of property in this kingdom that is not represented.

It appears then, that certain principles exist in the British constitution, which militate with each other; the reason of their doing so is evident; it was never supposed that they would extend beyond the limits of Great Britain, or affect so distant a country as America. It is much to be wished, therefore, that some expedient could be thought of to reconcile them.

The conduct of the several administrations that

have had the direction of the affairs of this kingdom, has been reciprocally arraigned; but, I think, without reason, for, all things considered, an impartial and dispassionate mind will find many excuses to allege in justification of each. —The fewest, I am afraid, are to be pleaded in favour of the Americans, for they settled in America under charters which expressly reserved to the British Parliament the authority, whether consistent or not consistent, now asserted. Although, therefore, they had a right to make humble representations to his majesty in Parliament, and to shew the impropriety and inconvenience of enforcing such principles, yet they had certainly no right to oppose them.

Expedients may still be found, it is to be hoped however, to conciliate the present unhappy differences, and restore harmony again between Great Britain and her colonies, but whatever measures may be adopted by Parliament, it is the duty and interest of America to submit.—But it is impertinent to enter any further into the discussion of a subject which is at this time under the deliberation of the supreme council of the nation. I will, therefore, conclude with a sincere prayer, that whatever measures may be adopted, they may be different in their issue from what the fears of men generally lead them to preconceive; and that, if they be coercive ones, they may be enforced, which, I am persuaded, is practicable, without the effusion of blood. if lenient ones, which are preferable, and which I think equally practicable, conceded without any loss or diminution of the dignity or interest of this kingdom.

Greenwich,
Jan. 29th, 1775.

TRAVELS

MIDDLE SETTLEMENTS

IN

NORTH AMERICA.

ON Friday the 27th of April, 1759, I embarked, in company with several North American gentlemen, on board the Dispatch, Captain Necks, for Virginia; and the next day we set sail from Spithead, under convoy of his majesty's ship the Lynn, Captain Sterling, commander, with thirty-three sail of trading vessels. We came to an anchor in the evening in Yarmouth Road, and the next day sailed with a fresh easterly wind through the Needles.

April 30. We passed by the Lizard, and in the evening discovered a sail, which proved to be an English sloop laden with corn. She had been taken by a French privateer, and was steering for France: there were three Frenchmen and one Englishman on board. The commodore sent some hands to her, with orders to carry her to Penzance.

May 1. Thick, hazy weather with a fair wind.

[29]

A large ship passed through the fleet about four o'clock in the afternoon: and in the evening another vessel bore down upon the sternmost ships, and spoke with them.

May 2. Fair, pleasant weather. The next day we found by our reckoning that we had made a hundred leagues from the Land's End.

May 4. Strong, violent gales at north-and-by-west. In the evening the Molly, Captain Chew, had her maintop-mast carried away, and hoisted a signal of distress.

May 5. From this time to the 14th, nothing remarkable happened: the wind was seldom fair, but the weather being moderate, we made frequent visits, and passed our time very agreeably.

May 14. Captain Necks fell ill of a fever, and continued indisposed several days: he began to mend about the 17th.

May 19. In the afternoon, a sudden and violent squall from the north-west obliged us to lie-to under our reefed main-sail: it continued to increase, and blew a storm for about thirty-six hours, when it began to moderate.

May 21. We made sail in the afternoon, with four ships in company; and the next day in the evening were joined by eighteen more. From that time to the 28th, nothing remarkable happened: we had generally pleasant weather, but adverse winds. We frequently visited; and were much entertained with seeing grampuses, turtles, bonetas, porpoises, flying and other fish, common in the Atlantic.*

May 28. We discovered a large sail; she directed her course towards the east. We supposed her to be an English man of war going express. She carried three top-gallant sails.

May 31. We spoke with a sloop bound from Antigua to London. She acquainted the commodore with the agreeable news of his majesty's forces at Guadaloupe having reduced that whole island under subjection to the British government. The wind still continued unfavourable.

June 5. We spoke with a snow from Carolina which informed the commodore that a French frigate was cruising off the capes of Virginia. From that time to the 11th, we had nothing remarkable. The wind was generally from west to north-west, and there were frequent squalls with lightning. We saw several bonetas, grampuses, albicores, and fish of different kinds.

June 11. The water appeared discoloured; and we concluded that we were upon the Banks of New-foundland: we cast the lead, but found no ground. The weather was thick and hazy. Nothing remarkable happened from this time to the 3d of July: we had pleasant weather, though now and then squalls with lightning. We fell in with several currents and had variable winds.

* See Appendix, No. 1

July 3. We had fine weather, with a gentle breeze at N. W. We were now, according to the commodore's reckoning (which we afterward found to be true) about sixty leagues from land. The air was richly scented with the fragrance of the pine-trees.

July 4. We saw a great many sloops, from whence we imagined that we were near the coast. The wind was at east-by-north

July 5. About six in the morning we caught some green fish: upon this we sounded, and found eighteen fathom water. At ten we discovered land, which proved to be Cape Charles; and about three hours afterward sailed through the capes into Chesapeake Bay. The commodore took his leave to go upon a cruise; and at eight in the evening we came to an anchor in York river, after a tedious and disagreeable voyage of almost ten weeks.

The next morning, having hired a chaise at York, a small inconsiderable town, I went to Williamsburg, about twelve miles distant. The road is exceedingly pleasant, through some of the finest tobacco plantations* in North America, with a beautiful view of the river and woods of great extent.

* The tobacco growing upon York river, is esteemed superior to any other in North America; particularly that which is raised upon the plantations belonging to Colonel Edward Diggs, which is said to have a flavour excelling all others. Of the growth of one plantation, distinguished from the rest, the tobacco is in such high estimation, that Colonel Diggs puts upon every hogshead in which it

Williamsburg, Virginia

Williamsburg is the capital of Virginia: it is situated between two creeks, one falling into James, the other into York river; and is built nearly due east and west.* The distance of each landing-place is something more than a mile from the town; which, with the disadvantage of not being able to bring up large vessels, is the reason of its not having increased so fast as might have been expected. It consists of about two hundred houses, does not contain more than one thousand souls, whites and negroes; and is far from being a place of any consequence. It is

is packed, the initials of his name, and it is from thence called the E. D. tobacco, and sells for a proportionably higher price. Some time ago, Colonel Diggs having a tract of land, seemingly of the same quality, and under the same exposure and aspect as the plantation producing the E. D. tobacco, from which it was separated only by a small rill of water, he directed it to be planted, and as the produce was apparently similar in quality, colour, flavour, and every other particular, he thought himself warranted to delineate E. D upon the hogsheads in which it was packed. Accordingly, it was sent to market with this recommendatory mark or token. But some time after, he received a letter from his factor or merchant in London, informing him that his inspector or agent had been guilty of some great oversight or error, as the tobacco contained in certain casks, which he specified, though marked with E. D., was of a different and very inferior quality to that commodity, and that if the same fault should be again committed, it would ruin the reputation and sale of the E. D. tobacco. It is to be observed, that the soil or mould had been carefully analysed and examined previous to its being planted, and that not the smallest difference could be perceived between that of the old and new plantation. The experiment, it will easily be believed, was not repeated.

* See Note I.

regularly laid out in parallel streets, intersected by others at right angles; has a handsome square in the center, through which runs the principal street, one of the most spacious in North America, three quarters of a mile in length, and above a hundred feet wide. At the opposite ends of this street are two public buildings, the college and the capitol· and although the houses are of wood, covered with shingles,* and but indifferently built, the whole makes a handsome appearance. There are few public edifices that deserve to be taken notice of; those, which I have mentioned, are the principal; and they are far from being magnificent. The governor's palace is tolerably good, one of the best upon the continent; but the church, the prison, and the other buildings, are all of them extremely indifferent. The streets are not paved, and are consequently very dusty, the soil hereabout consisting chiefly of sand: however, the situation of Williamsburg has one advantage which few or no places in these lower parts have, that of being free from mosquitoes. Upon the whole, it is an agreeable residence; there are ten or twelve gentlemen's families constantly residing in it, besides merchants and tradesmen: and at the times of the assemblies, and general courts, it is crowded with the gentry of the country: on those occasions there are balls and other

* These are formed in the shape of tiles, and are generally made of white cedar or of cypress.

amusements; but as soon as the business is finished, they return to their plantations; and the town is in a manner deserted.*

The situation of Virginia (according to Evans's map) is between the 36th and 40th degree of north lat. and about 76 degrees west long. from London.†
It is bounded on the north by the river Potomac, on the east by the Atlantic Ocean, by Carolina on the south, and, to include only what is inhabited, by the great Alleghany on the west.‡

The climate is extremely fine, though subject to violent heats in the summer: Fahrenheit's thermometer being generally for three months from 85 to 95 degrees high. The other seasons, however, make ample amends for this inconvenience: for the autumns and springs are delightful; and the winters are so mild and serene (though there are now and then excessively cold days) as scarcely to require a fire. The only complaint that a person can reasonably make, is, of the very sudden changes to which the weather is liable; for this being entirely regulated

* Since the revolution, the seat of government has been removed to Richmond, a town situated just below the falls of James river.

† Mr. Ebeling, of Hamburg, in a note to the German translation of this work, says, "Virginia is situated between 37 and 40 "degrees of north latitude, and extends from 77 to 81 degrees west "longitude from London," but I believe he is mistaken, for the latest and best maps generally agree with Mr. Evans in regard to the situation he has given to this country, at least, they approximate nearer to the account here given than to that of Mr. Ebeling.

‡ See Note II

by the winds, is exceedingly variable. Southerly winds are productive of heat, northerly of cold, and easterly of rain; whence it is no uncommon thing for the thermometer to fall many degrees in a very few hours; and, after a warm day to have such severe cold as to freeze over a river a mile broad in one night's time.* In summer there are frequent and violent gusts, with thunder and lightning; but as the country is very thinly inhabited, and most of the gentry have electrical rods to their houses, they are not attended with many fatal accidents. Now and then, indeed, some of the negroes lose their lives; and it is not uncommon in the woods to see trees torn and riven to pieces by their fury and violence. A remarkable circumstance happened some years ago at York, which is well attested: a person standing at his door during a thunder gust, was unfortunately killed; there was an intermediate tree at some distance, which was struck at the same time, and when they came to examine the body they found the tree delineated upon it in miniature. Part of the body was livid, but that which was covered by the tree was of its natural colour.†

I believe no country has more certainly proved

* On the 19th of December, 1759, being upon a visit to Colonel Washington, at Mount Vernon, upon the river Potomac, where the river is two miles broad, I was greatly surprised to find it entirely frozen over in the space of one night, when the preceding day had been mild and temperate.

† I have related this circumstance upon the authority of the

[36]

the efficacy of electrical rods, than this: before the discovery of them, these gusts were frequently productive of melancholy consequences; but now it is rare to hear of such instances. It is observable that no house was ever struck, where they were fixed: and although it has frequently happened that the rods themselves have been melted, or broken to pieces, and the houses scorched or discoloured along the sides of them, which manifested that they had received the stroke, but that the quantity of lightning was too great to be carried off by the conductor, yet never has any misfortune happened; such a direction having been given to the lightning as to prevent any danger or ill consequence. These circumstances, one would imagine, should induce every person to get over those prejudices which many have entertained; and to consider the neglect, rather than the use, of them as criminal, since they seem to be means put into our hands by Providence for our safety and protection.

The soil of Virginia is in general good. There are barrens where the lands produce nothing but pine trees; but taking the whole tract together, it is certainly fertile. The low grounds upon the rivers and creeks are exceedingly rich, being loam intermingled with sand: and the higher you go up into

Honourable John Blair, President of the Council of Virginia, who mentioned it as a well-known fact: but it appears so improbable and unphilosophical, that I do not pledge myself for the truth of it.

the country, towards the mountains, the value of the land increases; for it grows more strong, and consists of a deeper clay.

Virginia, in its natural state, produces great quantities of fruits and medicinal plants, with trees and flowers of infinitely various kinds. Tobacco and Indian corn are the original produce of the country; likewise the pigeon-berry, and rattle-snake-root so esteemed in all ulcerous and pleuritical complaints: grapes, strawberries, hickory nuts, mulberries, chestnuts, and several other fruits, grow wild and spontaneously.

Besides trees and flowers of an ordinary nature, the woods produce myrtles, cedars, cypresses, sugar-trees, firs of different sorts, and no less than seven or eight kinds of oak; they are likewise adorned and beautified with red-flowering maples, sassafras-trees, dog-woods, acacias, red-buds, scarlet-flowering chestnuts, fringe-trees, flowering poplars, umbrellas, magnolias, yellow jasamines, chamœdaphnes, pacoons, atamusco-lilies, May-apples, and innumerable other sorts, so that one may reasonably assert that no country ever appeared with greater elegance or beauty.*

Not to notice too the almost numberless creeks and rivulets which every where abound, it is watered by four large rivers of such safe navigation, and such noble and majestic appearance, as cannot be exceeded, perhaps, in the whole known world.

* See Appendix, No. 1.

Virginia

James river, which was formerly called Powhatan, from its having been the seat of that emperor, is seven miles broad at the mouth, navigable to the falls (above 150 miles) for vessels of large burden, and thence to the mountains for small craft and canoes.

The falls are in length about six or seven miles; they consist of innumerable breaks of water, owing to the obstruction of the current by an infinite number of rocks, which are scattered over the bed of the river; and form a most picturesque and beautiful cascade.

The Honourable Colonel Byrd,* has a small place called Belvedere, upon a hill at the lower end of these falls, as romantic and elegant as any thing I have ever seen. It is situated very high, and commands a fine prospect of the river, which is half a mile broad, forming cataracts in the manner above described, there are several little islands scattered carelessly about, very rocky, and covered with trees; and two or three villages† in view at a small distance. Over all these you discover a prodigious extent of wilderness, and the river winding majestically along through the midst of it.

York river, for about forty miles, to a place called West Point, is confined in one channel about two miles broad: it flows in a very direct course, making

* See Note III

† Amongst the rest, Richmond, the present seat of government.

[39]

but one angle, and that an inconsiderable one, during the whole way. At West Point it forks, and divides itself into two branches; the southward called Pamunky; the northward Mattapony: each of these branches, including the windings and meanders of the river, is navigable seventy or eighty miles, and a considerable way of this space for large ships.

The Rappahannock is navigable to the falls, which are a mile above Fredericksburg, and about 110 from the bay. Vessels of large burden may come up to this place; and small craft and canoes may be carried up much higher.

The Potomac is one of the finest rivers in North America: it is* ten miles broad at the mouth, navigable above 200 miles, to Alexandria, for men of war; and, allowing for a few carrying places, for canoes above 200 farther, to the very branches of the Ohio. Colonel Bouquet,† a Swiss gentleman in the Royal Americans, came down this autumn from Fort Cumberland‡ to Shenandoah with very little

* The Potomac, according to Mr. Jefferson, is only $7\frac{1}{2}$ miles broad at its mouth, and perhaps his account may be founded upon better authority than my own I had no opportunity of ascertaining the fact, and the statement which I have made rests entirely upon the credibility of those Virginian gentlemen, who favoured me with the information, and who, I am persuaded, did not intentionally mislead me, though it is possible they might be mistaken.

† See Note IV.

‡ The distance from Fort Cumberland to Shenandoah is above 100 miles; from Shenandoah to the great falls about 60, and from the great falls to Alexandria about 17 or 18

difficulty; whence to the great falls, I have been told, a navigation might easily be effected: so that this river seems to promise to be of as great consequence as any in North America.

In all these rivers the tide flows as far as the falls, and at Alexandria it rises between two and three feet. They discharge themselves into Chesapeake Bay, one of the finest in the world, which runs a great way up the country into Maryland; is from ten to twenty miles broad, navigable near a hundred leagues for vessels of almost any burden; and receives into its bosom at least twenty great rivers.

These waters are stored with incredible quantities of fish, such as sheeps-heads, rock-fish, drums, white perch, herrings, oysters, crabs, and several other sorts. Sturgeon and shad are in such prodigious numbers, that one day, within the space of two miles only, some gentlemen in canoes, caught above 600 of the former with hooks, which they let down to the bottom, and drew up at a venture when they perceived them to rub against a fish; and of the latter above 5,000 have been caught at one single haul of the seine.

In the mountains there are very rich veins of ore; some mines having been already opened which turn to great account; particularly Spotswood's iron mines* upon the Rappahannock, out of which they smelt annually above six hundred ton: and one of

* See Note V.

copper upon the Roanoke, belonging to Colonel Chiswell. This last mentioned gentleman is also going to try for lead upon some hunting-grounds belonging to the Indians, towards New River, and the Green Briar; where, it is said, there is fine ore, and in great plenty, lying above ground. Some coal mines have also been opened upon James river near the falls, which are likely to answer very well.

The forests abound with plenty of game of various kinds; hares, turkeys, pheasants, woodcocks, and partridges are in the greatest abundance. In the marshes are found soruses, a particular species of bird, more exquisitely delicious than the ortolan; snipes also, and ducks of various kinds. The American shell-drake and blue-wing exceed all of the duck kind whatsoever; and these are in prodigious numbers. In the woods there are variety of birds remarkable both for singing and for beauty; of which are the mocking-bird, the red-bird or nightingale, the blue-bird, the yellow-bird, the humming-bird*, the Baltimore bird, the summer-duck, the turtle, and several other sorts.

Insects and reptiles are almost innumerable. The variety of butterflies is not greater than is that of the

---

* The humming-bird is the smallest and most beautiful of all the feathered race. its colours are green, crimson, and gold; it lives chiefly by suction upon the sweets and essences of flowers, and nothing can be more curious than to observe numbers of them in gardens, where there are honey-suckles or trumpet-flowers, flying

rich and vivid colours with which each particular species is distinguished and beautified; and such is the number and appearance of the fire-flies, that on a summer's evening the whole air seems to glow and to be enlightened by them. Several snakes of this country are harmless and beautiful; such as the black snake, the wampum-snake, the bead-snake, the garter-snake, and some others: but the rattle-snake and vipers are exceedingly venomous and deadly. There are two curious species of frogs here: one is called the bull-frog, which is prodigiously large, and makes so loud a noise, that it may be heard at a great distance; the other is a small green frog, which sits upon the boughs of trees, and is found in almost every garden.

Of quadrupeds there are various kinds; squirrels of four or five different species*, opossums, raccoons, foxes, beavers, and deer: and in the deserts and un-inhabited parts, wolves, bears, panthers, elks or

and sucking out the sweetest juices The motion of their wings is incredibly swift and produces a humming noise, not unlike that of a large humble bee. They are frequently kept in cages, but seldom live longer than two months. The food which is given them, is either honey or sugar, mixed with water. Repeated attempts have been made to send them alive to England, but always without success.

* Of the several species of squirrels, the ground and flying squirrels are much the smallest and most beautiful. The former are of a dusky orange hue, streaked with black; the latter grey or ash-coloured, and elegantly formed. These have a spreading or fan-tail, and two membranes adhering to their sides, which, when they spring or leap from a tree, they expand, and are thereby en-

moose deer, buffaloes, mountain-cats, and various other sorts. Such are in general the natural productions of this country.*

Viewed and considered as a settlement, Virginia is far from being arrived at that perfection of which it is capable. Not a tenth of the land is yet cultivated: and that which is cultivated, is far from being so in the most advantageous manner. It produces, however, considerable quantities of grain and cattle, and fruit of many kinds. The Virginian pork is said to be superior in flavour to any in the world; but the sheep and horned cattle being small and lean, the meat of them is inferior to that of Great Britain, or indeed, of most parts of Europe. The horses are fleet and beautiful; and the gentlemen of Virginia, who are exceedingly fond of horse-racing, have spared no expence or trouble to improve the breed of them by importing great numbers from England.

The fruits introduced here from Europe succeed extremely well; particularly peaches, which have a very fine flavour, and grow in such plenty as to serve to feed the hogs in the autumn of the year. Their

abled to fly through a considerable space. The former are of a very wild nature; but these may be easily, and are frequently tamed. There is a species of polecat in this part of America, which is commonly called a skunk. This animal, when pursued, or assailed by its enemy, ejects its urine; which emits such a fetid and insupportable stench, as almost to stifle and suffocate whatever is within the reach of it.

* See Appendix, No. 1.

blossoms in the spring make a beautiful appearance throughout the country.

Virginia is divided into fifty-two counties, and seventy-seven parishes, and by act of assembly there ought to be forty-four towns*; but one half of these have not more than five houses; and the other half are little better than inconsiderable villages. This is owing to the cheapness of land, and the commodiousness of navigation: for every person may with ease procure a small plantation, can ship his tobacco at his own door, and live independent. When the colony shall come to be more thickly seated, and land grow dear, people will be obliged to follow trades and manufactures, which will necessarily make towns and large cities; but this seems remote, and not likely to happen for some centuries.

The inhabitants are supposed to be in number between two and three hundred thousand. There are a hundred and five thousand titheables, under which denomination are included all white males from sixteen to sixty; and all negroes whatsoever within the same age. The former are obliged to serve in the militia, and amount to forty thousand.

The trade of this colony is large and extensive. Tobacco is the principal article of it. Of this they export annually between fifty and sixty thousand hogsheads, each hogshead weighing eight hundred or a thousand weight, some years they export much

* These numbers have been since greatly increased.

more.* They ship also for the Madeiras, the Straits, and the West Indies, several articles, such as grain, pork, lumber, and cider: to Great Britain, bar-iron, indigo, and a small quantity of ginseng, though of an inferior quality; and they clear out one year with another about † ton of shipping.

Their manufactures are very inconsiderable They make a kind of cotton cloth, with which they clothe themselves in common, and call after the name of their country; and some inconsiderable quantities of linen, hose, and other trifling articles: but nothing to deserve attention.

The government is a royal one: the legislature consisting of a governor appointed by the king; a council of twelve persons, under the same nomination; and a house of burgesses, or representatives, of a hundred and eight or ten members, elected by the people; two for each county, and one for each of the following places, viz. the College of William and Mary, Jamestown, Norfolkborough, and Williamsburg. Each branch has a negative. All laws, in order to be permanent, must have the king's approbation; nor may any be enacted, which are repugnant to the laws of Great Britain.

The courts of judicature are either county, or general courts. The county courts are held monthly

* In the year 1758, it is said that seventy thousand hogsheads were exported.

† See Appendix, No 2.

in each county, at a place assigned for that purpose, by the justices thereof; four of them making a quorum. They are appointed by the governor, and take cognizance of all causes, at common law, or in chancery, within their respective counties, except criminal ones, punishable with loss of life, or member. This power they are not permitted to exercise except over negroes and slaves, and then not without a special commission from the governor for each particular purpose.* The general court is held twice a year at Williamsburg. It consists of the governor and council, any five of which make a court. They hear and determine all causes whatsoever, ecclesiastical or civil, and sit four and twenty days: the first five of these are for hearing and determining suits in chancery, appeals from the decrees of the county or inferior courts in chancery; and writs of supersedeas to such decrees. The other days are for trying suits or prosecutions in behalf of the king; and all other matters depending in the said court; appeals are allowed to the king in council, in cases

* How necessary it may be that they should have such a power, even in this case, I will not pretend to say, but the law which transfers it to them seems so inconsistent with the natural rights of mankind, that I cannot but in pity to humanity recite it

"Every slave committing any offence, by law punishable by "death, or loss of member, shall be committed to the county gaol, "and the sheriff of the county shall forthwith certify such com-"mitment, with the cause thereof, to the governor, or commander "in chief, who may issue a commission of oyer and terminer to "such persons as he shall think fit, which persons, forthwith after "the receipt of such commission, shall cause the offender to be of 500 l. sterling value. The governor has a power of pardoning criminals in all cases, except of treason or murder: and then he can only reprieve till he knows the king's pleasure.

The established religion is that of the Church of England; and there are very few Dissenters of any denomination in this province. There are at present between sixty and seventy clergymen; men in general of sober and exemplary lives. They have each a glebe of two or three hundred acres of land, a house, and a salary established by law of 16,000 weight of tobacco, with an allowance of 1,700 more for shrinkage. This is delivered to them in hogsheads ready packed for exportation, at the most convenient warehouse. The presentation of livings is in the hands of the vestry, which is a standing body of twelve members invested with the sole power of raising levies, settling the repairs of the church, and regulating other parochial business. They were originally elected by the people of the several parishes; but now fill up vacancies themselves. If the vestry does not present to a living in less than twelve months,

"publicly arraigned and tried at the court-house of the said county, "and take for evidence the confession of the offender, the oath of "one or more credible witnesses, or such testimony of negroes, "mulattoes or Indians, bond or free, with pregnant circumstances "as to them shall seem convincing, *without the solemnity of a jury*, "and the offender being found guilty, shall pass such judgment "upon him or her as the law directs for the like crimes, and on "such judgment award execution."
— Mercer's Abridgment of the Virginian Laws, p. 342

it lapses to the governor. The diocesan is the bishop of London; who has a power of appointing a commissary to preside over, and convene the clergy on particular occasions; and to censure, or even suspend them, in cases of neglect or immorality. His salary is 100 l. sterling per annum; and he is generally of the council, which is of equal emolument to him.*

An unhappy disagreement has lately arisen between the clergy and the laity, which, it is to be feared, may be of serious consequence. The cause of it was this: Tobacco being extremely scarce from a general failure of the crop, the assembly passed an act to oblige the clergy and all public officers to receive their stipends in money instead of tobacco. This the clergy remonstrated against, alleging the hardship of being obliged to take a small price for their tobacco, when it bore an extravagant one; seeing they never had any kind of compensation allowed when it was so plentiful as to be almost a drug. They sent over an agent to England, and the law was repealed. This greatly exasperated the people; and such is their mutual animosity at this time, that, I fear, it will not easily subside, or be forgotten.†

With regard to the law in question, it was certainly

* The commissary is commonly president of the college, and has the parish of Williamsburg, or some other lucrative parish, which render him about 350 l. a year· so that his annual income is between 5 and 600 l.

† See Note VI.

a very hard one; and I doubt whether, upon principles of free government, it can be justified; or whether the assembly can legally interpose any farther, than, in cases of necessity, to oblige the clergy to receive their salaries in money instead of tobacco, at the current price of tobacco. They may, I am persuaded, in cases of exigency, always make, and might then have made, such a law, without any considerable detriment to the colony: for, supposing the price of tobacco to be, what it was at that time, about fifty shillings currency per hundred, what would the whole sum be, were the clergy to be paid ad valorem? Not 20,200 l. sterling. There are in Virginia, as I observed before, about sixty-five clergymen; each of these is allowed 16,000 weight of tobacco; which, at the rate of fifty shillings currency per hundred, amounts to 400 l.; 400 l. multiplied by 65, is equal to 26,000; which, allowing 40 per cent. discount, the difference of exchange, is about 18,571 l. sterling. Now what is this sum to such a colony as Virginia? But to this it will be said, perhaps, why should the clergy be gainers in a time of public distress, when every one else is a sufferer? The clergy will doubtless reply, and why should the clergy be the only sufferers in plentiful seasons, when all but themselves are gainers? However, as on the one hand I disapprove of the proceedings of the assembly in this affair; so, on the other, I cannot approve of the steps which were taken

by the clergy: that violence of temper; that disre-
spectful behaviour towards the governor; that un-
worthy treatment of their commissary; and, to mention nothing else, that confusion of proceeding in
the convention, of which some, though not the ma-
jority, as has been invidiously represented, were
guilty; these things were surely unbecoming the
sacred character they are invested with; and the
moderation of those persons, who ought in all things
to imitate the conduct of their divine Master. If,
instead of flying out in invectives against the legislature; of accusing the governor of having given up
the cause of religion by passing the bill; when, in
fact, had he rejected it, he would never have been
able to have got any supplies during the course of
the war, though ever so much wanted; if, instead
of charging the commissary with want of zeal for
having exhorted them to moderate measures, they
had followed the prudent councils of that excellent
man, and had acted with more temper and moderation, they might, I am persuaded, in a very short
time, have obtained any redress they could reasonably have desired. The people in general were extremely well affected towards the clergy, and had
expressed their regard for them in several instances;
they were sensible, moreover, that their salaries
were too scanty to support them with dignity, and
there had been some talk about raising them: had
the clergy therefore, before they applied to England,

only offered a memorial to the assembly, setting forth that they thought the act extremely hard upon them, as their salaries were small; and that they hoped the assembly would take their case into consideration, and enable them to live with that decency which became their character; I am persuaded, from the knowledge which I have of the people in general, and from repeated conversations with several members of the assembly, that they might have obtained almost any thing they could have wished; if not, they undoubtedly would have had reason to appeal. But, instead of this, without applying to the assembly for relief, after the act was passed, (for before, indeed, some of them did apply to the speaker in private) they flew out into the most violent invectives, immediately sent over an agent to England, and appealed to his majesty in council. The result has been already related.

The progress of arts and sciences in this colony has been very inconsiderable: the college of William and Mary is the only public place of education, and this has by no means answered the design of its institution. It has a foundation for a president and six professors. The business of the president is to superintend the whole, and to read four theological lectures annually. He has a handsome house to live in, and 200 l. sterling per annum. The professor of the Indian school has 60 l. sterling, and a house also; his business is to instruct the Indians in reading, writing, and the principles of the Christian religion: this pious institution was set on foot and promoted by the excellent Mr. Boyle.*   The professor of humanity has the care of instructing the students in classical learning: he has an usher or assistant under him.   The four other professors teach moral philosophy, metaphysics, mathematics, and divinity.   Each of the professors has apartments in the college, and a salary of about 80 l. per annum.†   The present chancellor of the college is the bishop of London.

From what has been said of this colony, it will not be difficult to form an idea of the character‡ of its inhabitants.   The climate and external appearance of the country conspire to make them indolent, easy, and good natured; extremely fond of society,

* See Appendix, No. 3.

† They have since been raised, I believe, to 100 l.

‡ General characters are always liable to many exceptions.   In Virginia, I have had the pleasure to know several gentlemen adorned with many virtues and accomplishments, to whom the following description is by no means applicable.   Amongst others, I cannot resist the inclination of mentioning George Wythe, Esquire, who, to a perfect knowledge of the Greek language, which was taught him by his mother in the back woods, and of the ancient, particularly the Platonic philosophy, had joined such a profound reverence for the Supreme Being, such respect for the divine laws, such philanthropy for mankind, such simplicity of manners, and such inflexible rectitude and integrity of principle, as would have dignified a Roman senator, even in the most virtuous times of the republic.   This gentleman is, I believe, still living.¶

¶ See Note VII.

and much given to convivial pleasures. In consequence of this, they seldom show any spirit of enterprise, or expose themselves willingly to fatigue. Their authority over their slaves renders them vain and imperious, and entire strangers to that elegance of sentiment, which is so peculiarly characteristic of refined and polished nations. Their ignorance of mankind and of learning, exposes them to many errors and prejudices, especially in regard to Indians and negroes, whom they scarcely consider as of the human species; so that it is almost impossible, in cases of violence, or even murder, committed upon those unhappy people by any of the planters, to have the delinquents brought to justice for either the grand jury refuse to find the bill, or the petit jury bring in their verdict, not guilty.*

* There are two laws in this colony, which make it almost impossible to convict a planter, or white man, of the death of a negro or Indian. By the first it is enacted, that "if any slave shall die "by reason of any stroke or blow, given in correction by his or her "owner, or by reason of any accidental blow whatsoever, given "by such owner, no person concerned in such correction, or acci- "dental homicide, shall undergo any prosecution or punishment "for the same, unless, upon examination before the county court, "it shall be proved by the oath of one lawful and credible witness, "at least, that such slave was killed wilfully, maliciously, and de- "signedly; nor shall any person indicted for the murder of a slave, "and upon trial found guilty only of manslaughter, incur any for- "feiture or punishment for such offence or misfortune." See Mercer's Abridgment, p. 345. By the second, "No negro, "mulatto, or Indian, can be admitted into any court, or before "any magistrate, to be sworn as a witness, or give evidence in any "cause whatsoever, except upon the trial of a slave for a capital "offence." Mercer's Abridgment, p. 419.

Virginia

The display of a character thus constituted, will naturally be in acts of extravagance, ostentation, and a disregard of economy; it is not extraordinary therefore, that the Virginians outrun their incomes; and that having involved themselves in difficulties, they are frequently tempted to raise money by bills of exchange, which they know will be returned protested, with 10 per cent. interest.*

The public or political character of the Virginians corresponds with their private one: they are haughty and jealous of their liberties, impatient of restraint, and can scarcely bear the thought of being controuled by any superior power. Many of them consider the

---

* By an act of assembly, if any bill of exchange is drawn for the payment of any sum of money, and such bill is protested for non-payment, it carries interest from the date thereof, after the rate of 10 per cent, per annum, until the money be fully satisfied and paid.

A very curious anecdote relative to this law was mentioned to me at Williamsburg, of which I am persuaded the reader will excuse the relation. An usurer, not satisfied with 5 l. per cent. legal interest, refused to advance a sum of money to a gentleman, unless, by way of security, he would give him a bill of exchange that should be returned protested, by which he would be entitled to 10 per cent. The gentleman, who had immediate occasion for the money, drew a bill upon a capital merchant in London, with whom he had never had any transaction, or carried on the least correspondence. The merchant, on the receipt of the bill, observing the name of the drawer, very readily honoured it, knowing the gentleman to be a person of great property, and concluding that he meant to enter into correspondence with him. The usurer upon this became entitled to only 5 l per cent. He was exceedingly enraged, therefore, at being, as he supposed, thus tricked· and complained very heavily to the gentleman of his having given him a good bill instead of a bad one.

colonies as independent states, not connected with Great Britain, otherwise than by having the same common king, and being bound to her by natural affection. There are but few of them that have a turn for business, and even those are by no means expert at it. I have known them, upon a very urgent occasion, vote the relief of a garrison, without once considering whether the thing was practicable, when it was most evidently and demonstrably otherwise.* In matters of commerce they are ignorant of the necessary principles that must prevail between a colony and the mother country; they think it a hardship not to have an unlimited trade to every part of the world. They consider the duties upon their staple as injurious only to themselves;

---

* The garrison here alluded to, was that of Fort Loudoun, in the Cherokee country, consisting of a lieutenant, and about fifty men. This unfortunate party being besieged by the Cherokee Indians, and reduced to the last extremity, sent off runners to the governors of Virginia and Carolina, imploring immediate succour; adding, that it was impossible for them to hold out above twenty days longer. The assembly of Virginia, commiserating their unhappy situation, very readily voted a considerable sum for their relief. With this, troops were to be levied, were to rendezvous upon the frontiers 200 miles distant from Williamsburg; were afterward to proceed to the fort 200 miles farther through a wilderness, where there was no road, no magazines, no posts, either to shelter the sick, or cover a retreat in case of any disaster, so that the unfortunate garrison might as effectually have been succoured from the moon. The author taking notice of these difficulties to one of the members, he frankly replied, " Faith, it is true: but we have had an opportunity at least of showing our loyalty." In a few days after arrived the melancholy news, that this unfortunate party was entirely cut off.

and it is utterly impossible to persuade them that they affect the consumer also. However, to do them justice, the same spirit of generosity prevails here which does in their private character; they never refuse any necessary supplies for the support of government when called upon, and are a generous and loyal people.

The women are, generally speaking, handsome, though not to be compared with our fair country-women in England. They have but few advantages, and consequently are seldom accomplished; this makes them reserved, and unequal to any interesting or refined conversation. They are immoderately fond of dancing, and indeed it is almost the only amusement they partake of: but even in this they discover want of taste and elegance, and seldom appear with that gracefulness and ease, which these movements are calculated to display. Towards the close of an evening, when the company are pretty well tired with country dances, it is usual to dance jigs; a practice originally borrowed, I am informed, from the negroes.* These dances are without method or regularity: a gentleman and lady stand up, and dance about the room, one of them retiring, the other pursuing, then perhaps meeting, in an irregular fantastical manner. After some

* The author has since had an opportunity of observing something similar in Italy. The trescone of the Tuscans is very like the jigs of the Virginians.

time, another lady gets up, and then the first lady must sit down, she being, as they term it, cut out: the second lady acts the same part which the first did, till somebody cuts her out. The gentlemen perform in the same manner. The Virginian ladies, excepting these amusements, and now and then going upon a party of pleasure into the woods to partake of a barbecue,* chiefly spend their time in sewing and taking care of their families: they seldom read, or endeavour to improve their minds; however, they are in general good housewives; and though they have not, I think, quite so much tenderness and sensibility as the English ladies, yet they make as good wives, and as good mothers, as any in the world.

It is hard to determine whether this colony can be called flourishing, or not; because though it produces great quantities of tobacco and grain, yet there seem to be very few improvements carrying on in it. Great part of Virginia is a wilderness, and as

---

* Mons. de Wılld, in his French translation of these travels, makes the following observation upon the word, barbecue:

"Cet amusement barbare consiste a fouetter les porcs jusqu'a "la mort, pour en rendre la chair plus delicate. Je ne sache pas "que les cannibales même le pratiquent"

In justice to the inhabitants of Virginia, I must beg leave to observe, that such a cruel and inhuman act was never, to my knowledge at least, practised in that country. A barbecue is nothing more than a porker, killed in the usual way, stuffed with spices and other rich ingredients, and basted with Madeira wine. It is esteemed a very great delicacy; and is, I believe, a costly dish.

many of the gentlemen are in possession of immense
tracts of land, it is likely to continue so. A spirit
of enterprise is by no means the turn of the colony,
and therefore few attempts have been made to force
a trade; which I think might easily be done, both to
the West Indies and the Ohio. They have every
thing necessary for such an undertaking; viz. lumber,
provisions, grain, and every other commodity, which
the other colonies, that subsist and grow rich by
these means, make use of for exports; but, instead of
this, they have only a trifling communication with
the West Indies; and as to the Ohio, they have suffered themselves, notwithstanding the superior advantages they might enjoy from having a water
carriage almost to the Youghiogheny, to neglect this
valuable branch of commerce; while the industrious
Pennsylvanians seize every opportunity, and struggle
with innumerable difficulties to secure it to themselves. The Virginians are content if they can but
live from day to day; they confine themselves almost
entirely to the cultivation of tobacco; and if they have
but enough of this to pay their merchants in London,
and to provide for their pleasures, they are satisfied,
and desire nothing more. Some few, indeed, have
been rather more enterprising, and have endeavoured to improve their estates by raising indigo, and
other schemes: but whether it has been owing to the
climate, to their inexperience in these matters, or
their want of perseverance, I am unable to deter-

mine, but their success has not answered their expectations.

The taxes of this colony are considerable, and the
public debt amounts to at least 400,000 l. currency;
this they have been driven into by the war, having
seldom had less than a thousand or fifteen hundred
provincial troops in pay, exclusive of the expenses
of some forts. The ways and means employed for
raising the money have been generally the same:
they have first made an emission of so much paper
currency as the exigency required, and then laid a
tax for sinking it. This tax has been commonly
upon lands and negroes, two shillings for every
titheable; and a shilling or eighteen-pence upon
every hundred acres of land. This mode of taxa-
tion has occasioned some divisions in the house; for
the owners of large tracts being unable, perhaps, to
cultivate a tenth part of their possessions, and every
man's real income arising from the number of his
negroes, have thought it very hard to pay a tax for
what they pretend is of no value to them: but much
better arguments may undoubtedly be urged in support of the tax than against it.

The taxes for the present debt are laid till the
year sixty-nine, when the whole, if they add nothing
more to it, will be discharged. The use of paper
currency in this colony has entirely banished from
it gold and silver. Indeed, the introduction of it
was certain in time to produce this effect; but lest

it should not, the Virginians fell into a measure, which completed it at once: for by an act of assembly they fixed the exchange between currency and sterling debts at five and twenty per cent. not considering that the real value of their currency could only be regulated by itself. The consequence was, that when from frequent emissions, the difference of exchange between bills upon merchants in London and currency was 40 per cent., the difference between currency and specie* was only five and twenty. So that the moneyed men collected all the specie they could, sent it to Philadelphia, where it passed for its real value, purchased bills of exchange with it there, and sold them again in Virginia with fifteen per cent. profit: and this they continued to do till there was not a pistole or a dollar remaining.

During my stay in Virginia, I made several excursions into different parts of the country: one in particular to the great falls of Potomac; of which, as I expected to be highly entertained, I kept a journal.

I departed from Williamsburg, Oct. 1, 1759, in company with another gentleman;† and we travelled that day about forty miles, to a plantation‡ in King

---

* Fixing the difference between currency and sterling debts, was, in reality, fixing it between currency and specie.

† Col. Bernard Moore.

‡ Belonging to Col. Symes. This gentleman's lady, a very beautiful woman, was said to have just attained her 21st year.

William county, beautifully situated upon a high hill, on the north side of Pamunky river. A little below this place stands the Pamunky Indian town, where at present are the few remaining of that large tribe, the rest having dwindled away through intemperance and disease. They live in little wigwams or cabins upon the river; and have a very fine tract of land of about 2,000 acres, which they are restrained from alienating by act of assembly Their employment is chiefly hunting or fishing for the neighboring gentry. They commonly dress like the Virginians, and I have sometimes mistaken them for the lower sort of that people.* The night I spent here, they went out into an adjoining marsh to catch soruses; and one of them, as I was informed in the morning, caught near a hundred dozen. The manner of taking these birds is remarkable. The sorus is not known to be in Virginia, except for about six weeks from the latter end of September: at that time they are found in the marshes in prodigious numbers, feeding upon the wild oats. At first they are exceedingly lean, but in a short time grow so fat, as to be unable to fly: in this state they lie upon the reeds, and the Indians go out in canoes and knock them on the head with their paddles. They are

She was at that time the mother of seven children, all living. The women in general, in this country, arrive at maturity very early. Some are marriageable at eleven, many at thirteen, and the generality at fourteen or fifteen years of age.

* See Appendix, No. 3.

rather bigger than a lark, and are delicious eating. During the time of their continuing in season, you meet with them at the tables of most of the planters, breakfast, dinner and supper.*

Oct. 2. We went to another plantation about twenty-four miles distant, belonging to a private gentleman,† upon Mattapony river. We staid there all that and the next day on account of rain.

Oct. 4. We traveled twenty-five miles to another gentleman's ‡ house; and from thence, the day following, about twenty-five miles farther, to a town called Fredericksburg.

Fredericksburg is situated about a mile below the Falls of Rappahannock: it is regularly laid out, as most of the towns in Virginia are, in parallel streets. Part of it is built upon an eminence, and commands a delightful prospect; the rest upon the edge of the water for the convenience of warehouses. The town was begun about thirty-two years ago, for the sake of carrying on a trade with the back-settlers; and is at present by far the most flourishing one in these parts.

* In several parts of Virginia the ancient custom of eating meat at breakfast still continues. At the top of the table, where the lady of the house presides, there is constantly tea and coffee; but the rest of the table is garnished with roasted fowls, ham, venison, game, and other dainties. Even at Williamsburg, it is the custom to have a plate of cold ham upon the table; and there is scarcely a Virginian lady who breakfasts without it.

† Major Henry Gaines.

‡ Col Bailors.

[63]

We left Fredericksburg the 6th instant, and went to see the Falls. At this place is a small mercantile town called Falmouth, whose inhabitants are endeavouring to rival the Fredericksburghers in their trade. It is built upon the north side of the river, and consists of eighteen or twenty houses.

The Falls of Rappahannock are similar to those of James river, except that they are not upon so large a scale. The whole range scarcely exceeds half a mile, and the breadth not a hundred yards. At the time of our going to see them, there was a fresh in the river, which added very much to their beauty. The center of view was an island of about an hundred acres covered with trees; this divided the river into two branches, in each of which, at regular distances of fifteen or twenty yards, was a chain of six or seven falls, one above another, the least of them a foot perpendicular. The margin was beautifully variegated with rocks and trees, and the whole formed a pleasing romantic scene.

At this place we met with a person who informed us of his having been, a few days before, a spectator of that extraordinary phenomenon in nature, the fascinating power of the rattle-snake. He observed one lying coiled near a tree, looking directly at a bird which had settled there. The bird was under great agitation, uttered the most doleful cries, hopped from spray to spray, and at length flew directly down to the snake, which opened its mouth and swallowed it.

The Northern Neck

From hence we ascended up the river, about fifteen miles, to Spotswood's iron-mines; and in our way had a fine view of the Appalachian mountains, or Blue Ridge, at the distance of seventy miles. At this place I was much affected by the following incident. A gentleman in our company, which was now increased, had a small negro boy with him, about fourteen years of age, that had lived with him in a remote part of the country some time as a servant; an old woman who was working in the mines, and who proved to be the boy's grandmother, accidentally cast her eyes on him; she viewed him with great attention for some time; then screamed out, saying that it was her child, and flung herself down upon the ground. She lay there some seconds; rose up, looked on him again in an ecstasy of joy, and fell upon his neck and kissed him. After this, she retired a few paces, examined him afresh with fixed attention, and immediately seemed to lose herself in thoughtful and profound melancholy. The boy all this while stood silent and motionless, reclining his head on one side, pale and affected beyond description. It would not have been in the power of painting to exhibit a finer picture of distress.

We returned from this place the next day to Fredericksburg; and ferrying over the Rappahannock into the Northern Neck, travelled about seventeen miles to a gentleman's house in Stafford county: in the morning we proceeded through Dumfries, and over Occoquan river to Colchester, about twenty-one miles.

These are two small towns lately built for the sake of the back trade; the former* on the Quantico, the other upon Occoquan river, both of which fall into the Potomac. About two miles above Colchester there is an iron furnace, a forge, two saw-mills, and a bolting-mill: at our return we had an opportunity of visiting them: they have every convenience of wood and water, that can be wished for. The ore wrought here is brought from Maryland; not that there is any doubt of there being plenty enough in the adjacent hills; but the inhabitants are discouraged from trying for it by the proprietor's (viz. Lord Fairfax) having reserved to himself a third of all ore that may be discovered in the Northern Neck.†

* In the preceding editions of this book, Dumfries is mentioned as situated upon Acquia Creek but this is certainly erroneous, for all the maps describe it as situated upon the Quantico The error probably arose from the author's having passed the Acquia, the Quantico, and the Occoquan rivers in the same day, and his want of perfect and correct recollection, when he wrote his journal in the evening.

† An occurrence happened to me in the course of this day's travelling, which, though it made a considerable impression upon me at the time, I should not have thought of sufficient moment to be recorded, had not the intellectual powers of the African negroes been frequently, of late, made the subject of conversation, both by the friends and the opposers of the emancipation of that unhappy race. In passing either Acquia, Quantico, or Occoquan rivers, I do not recollect which, I was rowed by an old gray-headed negro who seemed quite exhausted and worn down by age and infirmity. I inquired into his situation, and received for answer, that he had

Falls of Potomac

From Colchester we went about twelve miles farther to Mount Vernon. This place is the property of Colonel Washington, and truly deserving of its owner.* The house is most beautifully situated upon a high hill on the banks of the Potomac; and commands a noble prospect of water, of cliffs, of woods, and plantations. The river is nearly two miles broad, though two hundred from the mouth;

been a slave from his youth, and had continued to work for his master till age had rendered him unfit for service; that his master had then kindly given him a small piece of ground, and the profits of the ferry, which were indeed very inconsiderable, for his maintenance; and that with these means of subsistence he awaited the hour when it might please God to call him to another life. I observed that he must naturally wish for that hour, as it would release him from his present sufferings. His answer was, no, for he was afraid to die. On my questioning him, why he was afraid to die: whether he had any thing upon his conscience that gave him uneasiness; or whether he had not been honest and faithful to his master? He answered, yes, I have always done my duty to the best of my power. but yet I am afraid to die· and was not our Saviour himself afraid to die? The answer was so unexpected, and so far beyond what I supposed to be the intellectual capacity of the poor negro, that it sunk deep into my mind, and I was lost for a moment in silence.

* I cannot omit this opportunity of bearing testimony to the gallant and public spirit of this gentleman. Nov. 1, 1753, Lieut. Gov. Dinwiddie having informed the assembly of Virginia, that the French had erected a fort upon the Ohio, it was resolved to send somebody to M St Pierre, the commander, to claim that country as belonging to his Britannic Majesty, and to order him to withdraw. Mr. Washington, a young gentlemen of fortune just arrived at age, offered his service on this important occasion. The distance was more than 400 miles; 200 of which lay through a trackless desert, inhabited by cruel and merciless savages, and the season was uncommonly severe. Notwithstanding these dis-

and divides the dominions of Virginia from Maryland.* We rested here one day, and proceeded up
the river about twenty-six miles, to take a view of the
Great Falls. These are formed in some respect like
those of the Rappahannock; but are infinitely more
noble. The channel of the river is contracted by
hills; and is as narrow, I was told, as at Fort Cumberland, which is an hundred and fifty miles higher
up. It is clogged moreover with innumerable rocks;
so that the water for a mile or two flows with ac-
celerated velocity. At length coming to a ledge of
rocks, which runs diametrically across the river, it
divides into two spouts, each about eight yards wide,

couraging circumstances, Mr. Washington, attended by one companion only, set out upon this dangerous enterprise travelled
from Winchester on foot, carrying his provisions on his back, executed his commission, and after incredible hardships, and many
providential escapes, returned safe to Williamsburg, and gave an
account of his negotiation to the assembly, the 14th day of February following.

* A very curious sight is frequently exhibited upon this and the
other great rivers in Virginia, which for its novelty is exceedingly
diverting to strangers. During the spring and summer months
the fishing-hawk is often seen hovering over the rivers, or resting
on the wing without the least visible change of place for some
minutes, then suddenly darting down and plunging into the water,
from whence it seldom rises again without a rock fish, or some
other considerable fish, in its talons. It immediately shakes off the
water like a mist, and makes the best of its way towards the woods.
The bald eagle, which is generally upon the watch, instantly pur-
sues, and if it can overtake, endeavours to soar above it. The
hawk growing solicitous for its own safety drops the fish, and the
bald eagle immediately stoops, and seldom fails to catch it in its
pounces before it reaches the water.

and rushes down a precipice with incredible rapidity. The spout on the Virginian side makes three falls, one above another; the first about ten feet, the next fifteen, and the last twenty-four or twenty-five feet perpendicular: the water is of a vast bulk, and almost entire. The spout on the Maryland side is nearly equal in height and quantity, but a great deal more broken. These two spouts, after running in separate channels for a short space, at length unite in one about thirty yards wide; and as we judged from the smoothness of the surface and our unsuccessful endeavours to fathom it, of prodigious depth. The rocks on each side are at least ninety or a hundred feet high; and yet, in great freshes, the water overflows the tops of them, as appeared by several large and entire trees, which had lodged there.

In the evening we returned down the river about sixteen miles to Alexandria, or Belhaven, a small trading place in one of the finest situations imaginable. The Potomac above and below the town, is not more than a mile broad, but it here opens into a large circular bay, of at least twice that diameter.

The town is built upon an arc of this bay; at one extremity of which is a wharf; at the other a dock for building ships; with water sufficiently deep to launch a vessel of any rate or magnitude.

The next day we returned to Colonel Washington's, and in a few days afterward to Williamsburg.

The time of my residence in this colony was ten

months, and I received so many instances of friendship and good-nature, that not to acknowledge them
would be an act of ingratitude. It would not be
easy to mention particular instances, without being
guilty of injustice by omitting others: but, in general,
I can truly affirm, that I took leave of this hospitable
people with regret, and shall ever remember them
with gratitude and affection.

May 26, 1760. Having procured three horses,
for myself, servant, and baggage, I departed from
Williamsburg, and travelled that night to Eltham;*
twenty-five miles.

May 27. I ferried over Pamunky river at Dan-
sies, and went to Todd's ordinary upon Mattopony,
or the northern branch of York river; thirty-two
miles.

May 28. I went to a plantation in Caroline
county;† twenty-seven miles.

May 29. To Fredericksburg; twenty-five miles.

As I was travelling this day, I observed a large
black-snake, about six feet long, lying cross the stump
of a tree by the road side. I touched it with my
switch several times before it stirred; at last it darted
with incredible swiftness into the woods. On looking into the hole, where it had fixed its head, I
observed a small bead-snake about two feet long; beautifully variegated with red, black, and orange colour,

* The plantation of Col. Bassett

† Belonging to Col. Bailor, mentioned above.

[70]

which the black-snake was watching to prey upon. I took and laid it, half stupefied, in the sun to revive. After I proceeded about a quarter of a mile, it occurred to me that it would be a great curiosity if I could carry it to England; I therefore sent my servant back with orders to fetch it. but, at his return, he acquainted me that it was not to be found, and that the black-snake was in the same position wherein I had first discovered it. I mention this as an instance of the intrepid nature of the black-snake, which, though not venomous, will attack and devour the rattlesnake; and, in some cases, it is asserted, even dare to assault a man.

May 30. I left Fredericksburg, and having ferried over the Rappahannock at the falls, travelled that night to Neville's ordinary, about thirty-four miles.

May 31. I passed over the Pignut and Blue Ridges; and, crossing the Shenandoah, arrived, after a long day's journey of above fifty miles, at Winchester.*

The Pignut ridge is a continuation of the southwest mountains. It is no where very high; and at the gap where I passed, the ascent is so extremely easy, owing to the winding of the road between the mountains, that I was scarcely sensible of it.

* Greenway Court, the seat of the venerable Lord Fairfax, is situated a few miles on the left of the road, about half way between the Appalachian mountains and Winchester. His Lordship being absent, I was prevented from paying my respects to him.—See Appendix, No. 4.

The tract of country lying between this ridge and the coast, is supposed, and with some appearance of probability, to have been gained from the ocean. The situation is extremely low, and the ground every where broken into small hills, nearly of the same elevation, with deep intermediate gullies, as if it were the effect of some sudden retiring of the waters. The soil is principally of sand; and there are few, if any pebbles, within a hundred miles of the shore; for which reason the Virginians in these parts never shoe their horses. Incredible quantities of what are called scallop-shells are found also near the surface of the ground; and many of the hills are entirely formed of them. These phenomena, with others less obvious to common observation, seem to indicate that the Atlantic, either gradually, or by some sudden revolution in nature, has retired, and lost a considerable part of that dominion which formerly belonged to it.

The Blue Ridge is much higher than the Pignut: though even these mountains are not to be compared with the Alleghany. To the southward, I was told, they are more lofty; and but little, if at all, inferior to them The pass, at Ashby's Gap, from the foot of the mountain on the eastern side to the Shenandoah, which runs at the foot on the western, is about four miles. The ascent is no where very steep; though the mountains are, upon the whole, I think, higher than any I have ever seen in England. When I got

[72]

to the top, I was inexpressibly delighted with the scene which opened before me. Immediately under the mountain, which was covered with chamœdaphnes in full bloom, was a most beautiful river: beyond this an extensive plain, diversified with every pleasing object that nature can exhibit; and, at the distance of fifty miles, another ridge of still more lofty mountains, called the Great, or North Ridge,* which inclosed and terminated the whole.

The river Shenandoah rises a great way to the southward from under this Great North Ridge. It runs through Augusta county, and falls into the Potomac somewhere in Frederick At the place where I ferried over, it is only about a hundred yards wide; and indeed it is no where, I believe, very broad. It is exceedingly romantic and beautiful, forming great variety of falls, and is so transparent, that you may see the smallest pebble at the depth of eight or ten feet. There is plenty of trout and other fish in it; but it is not navigable, except for rafts In sudden freshes it rises above forty or fifty feet. The low grounds upon the banks of this river are very rich and fertile; they are chiefly settled by Germans, who gain a comfortable livelihood by raising stock for the troops, and sending butter down into the lower parts of the country. I could not but reflect with pleasure on the situation of these people; and think

* All these ridges consist of single mountains joined together, and run parallel to each other

if there is such a thing as happiness in this life, that they enjoy it. Far from the bustle of the world, they live in the most delightful climate, and richest soil imaginable; they are everywhere surrounded with beautiful prospects and sylvan scenes; lofty mountains, transparent streams, falls of water, rich valleys, and majestic woods; the whole interspersed with an infinite variety of flowering shrubs, constitute the landscape surrounding them: they are subject to few diseases; are generally robust; and live in perfect liberty: they are ignorant of want, and acquainted with but few vices. Their inexperience of the elegancies of life precludes any regret that they possess not the means of enjoying them: but they possess what many princes would give half their dominions for, health, content, and tranquillity of mind.

Winchester is a small town of about two hundred houses. It is the place of general rendezvous of the Virginian troops, which is the reason of its late rapid increase, and present flourishing condition. The country about it, before the reduction of Fort du Quesne, was greatly exposed to the ravages of the Indians, who daily committed most horrid cruelties: even the town would have been in danger, had not Colonel Washington, in order to cover and protect it, erected a fort upon an eminence at one end of it, which proved of the utmost utility; for although the Indians were frequently in sight of the town, they

[74]

never dared to approach within reach of the fort. It is a regular square fortification, with four bastions, mounting twenty-four cannon; the length of each curtain, if I am not mistaken, is about eighty yards. Within, there are barracks for 450 men. The materials of which it is constructed are logs filled up with earth· the soldiers attempted to surround it with a dry ditch; but the rock was so extremely hard and impenetrable that they were obliged to desist. It is still unfinished; and, I fear, going to ruin; for the assembly, who seldom look a great way before them, after having spent about 9,000 l. currency upon it, cannot be prevailed upon to give another thousand towards finishing it, because we are in possession of Pittsburg; and, as they suppose, quite secure on this account; yet it is certain, that, in case of another Indian war on this side, which is by no means improbable, considering our general treatment of that people, it would be of the utmost advantage and security.

There is a peculiarity in the water at Winchester, owing, I was told, to the soil's being of a limy quality, which is frequently productive of severe gripings, especially in strangers; but it is generally supposed, on the other hand, to be specific against some other diseases.*

* Professor Haller, in his notes to the German translation of this book, supposes that the water at Winchester may be impregnated with Vitriolic Magnesia, Sal Amarum.

During my stay at this place, I was almost induced to make a tour for a fortnight to the southward, in Augusta county, for the sake of seeing some natural curiosities, which, the officers assured me, were extremely well worth visiting: but as the Cherokees had been scalping in those parts only a few days before; and as I feared, at the same time, that it would detain me too long, and that I should lose my passage to England, I judged it prudent to decline it.

The curiosities they mentioned to me, were chiefly these:

1. About forty miles westward of Augusta courthouse, a beautiful cascade, bursting out of the side of a rock; and, after running some distance through a meadow, rushing down a precipice 150 feet perpendicular.

2. To the southward of this about twenty miles, two curious hot springs, one tasting like alum, the other like the washings of a gun.

3. A most extraordinary cave.

4. A medicinal spring, specific in venereal cases. A soldier in the Virginian regiment, whose case was thought desperate, by drinking and bathing in these waters, was, after a few days, entirely cured. This fact was asserted very strongly by some officers, who had been posted there: but Colonel Washington, of whom I inquired more particularly concerning it, informed me that he had never heard of it; that he

was not indeed at the place where it is said to have happened, but that having had the command of the regiment at that time, he should probably have been informed of it. What credit therefore is to be given to it, the reader must judge for himself.

5. Sixty miles southward of Augusta court-house, a natural arch, or bridge, joining two high mountains, with a considerable river running underneath.

6. A river called Lost river, from its sinking under a mountain, and never appearing again.

7. A spring of a sulphurous nature, an infallible cure for particular cutaneous disorders.

8. Sixteen miles north-east of Winchester, a natural cave or well, into which, at times, a person may go down to the depth of 100 or 150 yards; and at other times the water rises up to the top, and overflows plentifully. This is called the ebbing and flowing well, and is situated in a plain, flat country, not contiguous to any mountain or running water.

9. A few miles from hence, six or seven curious caves communicating with each other.

A day or two before I left Winchester, I discovered that I had been robbed by my servant: he confessed the fact, and pleaded so little in justification of himself, that I was obliged to dismiss him. This distressed me very much, for it was impossible to hire a servant in these parts, or even any one to go over the mountains with me into the lower settlements. However, by the politeness of the commander of the place, the Honourable Colonel Byrd, and of another gentleman* of my acquaintance, I got over these difficulties; for the former, while I continued at Winchester, accommodated me with his own apartments in the fort, ordering his servants to attend and wait upon me; and the latter sent a negro boy with me as far as Colonel Washington's, eighty miles distant from this place. On the 4th of June, therefore, I was enabled to leave Winchester, and I travelled that night about eighteen miles, to Sniker's† ferry upon the Shenandoah.

The next morning I repassed the Blue Ridge at William's Gap, and proceeded on my journey about forty miles. I this day fell into conversation with a planter, who overtook me on the road, concerning the rattle-snake, of which there are infinite numbers in these parts; and he told me, that one day going to a mill at some distance, he provoked one to such a degree, as to make it strike a small vine which grew close by, and that the vine presently drooped and died.‡

My accommodations this evening were extremely

* Colonel Churchill.

† Called in Fry and Jefferson's map, Williams's Ferry.

‡ Several persons to whom I have mentioned this fact, have seemed to doubt of the probability of it. But were it not true, a question will naturally arise, how an idea of that nature should occur to an ignorant planter, living remote from all cultivated society, and, more particularly, how he should happen to fix upon that tree, which, supposing the thing possible, is the most likely to have been affected in the manner described.

[78]

bad; I had been wet to the skin in the afternoon; and at the miserable plantation in which I had taken shelter, I could get no fire; nothing to eat or drink but pure water; and not even a blanket to cover me. I threw myself down upon my mattrass, but suffered so much from cold, and was so infested with insects and vermin, that I could not close my eyes. I rose early in the morning, therefore, and proceeded upon my journey, being distant from Colonel Washington's not more than thirty miles. It was late, however, before I arrived there, for it rained extremely hard, and a man who undertook to shew me the nearest way, led me among precipices and rocks, and we were lost for above two hours. It was not, indeed, without some compensation; for he brought me through as beautiful and picturesque a scene, as eye ever beheld. It was a delightful valley, about two miles in length, and a quarter of one in breadth, between high and craggy mountains, covered with chamœdaphnes* or wild ivy, in full flower   Through the middle of the valley glided a rivulet about eight yards wide, extremely lucid, and breaking into innumerable cascades; and in different parts of it stood

* The chamœdaphne is the most beautiful of all flowering shrubs Catesby in his Natural History of Carolina speaks of it in the following manner "The flowers grow in bunches on the "tops of the branches, to footstalks of three inches long, they are "white, stained with purplish red; consisting of one leaf in form "of a cup, divided at the verge into five sections   In the middle "is a stilus, and ten stamina, which, when the flower first opens, " appear lying close to the sides of the cup, at equal distances, their

small clumps of evergreens, such as myrtles, cedars, pines, and various other sorts. Upon the whole, not Tempe itself could have displayed greater beauty or a more delightful scene.

At Colonel Washington's I disposed of my horses, and, having borrowed his curricle and servant, I took leave of Mount Vernon the 11th of June

I crossed over the Potomac into Maryland at Clifton's ferry, where the river is something more than a mile broad; and proceeded on my journey to Marlborough, eighteen miles. I here met with a strolling company of players, under the direction of one Douglas. I went to see their theatre, which was a neat, convenient tobacco-house, well fitted up for the purpose.* From hence in the afternoon I proceeded to Queen Anne, nine miles; and in the evening nine miles farther, over the Patuxent to Londontown ferry; I staid here all night, and early in the morning ferrying over South river, three quarters of a mile in breadth, I arrived at Annapolis, four miles distant, about nine in the morning.

Annapolis is the capital of Maryland; it is a small, neat town, consisting of about a hundred and fifty

"apices being lodged in ten little hollow cells, which being promi-"nent on the outside, appear as so many little tubercles.—As all "plants have their peculiar beauties, it is difficult to assign to any "one an elegance excelling all others, yet considering the curious "structure of the flower, and beautiful appearance of this whole "plant, I know of no shrub that has a better claim to it." Catesby, Vol. II. p. 98. See Appendix, No 1.

* See Note VIII.

houses, situated on a peninsula upon Severn river.
The peninsula is formed by the river, and two small
creeks; and although the river is not above a mile
broad; yet as it falls into Chesapeake bay a little below, there is from this town the finest water-prospect
imaginable. The bay is twelve miles over, and beyond it you may discern the eastern shore; so that
the scene is diversified with fields, woods, and water.
The tide rises here about two feet, and the water is
salt, though the distance of the Capes is more than
200 miles. The town is not laid out regularly, but
is tolerably well built, and has several good brick
houses. None of the streets are paved, and the few
public buildings here are not worth mentioning.
The church is a very poor one, the stadt-house but
indifferent, and the governor's palace is not finished.
This last mentioned building was begun a few years
ago, it is situated very finely upon an eminence, and
commands a beautiful view of the town and environs.
It has four large rooms on the lower floor, besides
a magnificent saloon, a stair-case, and a vestibule.
On each side of the entrance are four windows, and
nine upon the first story; the offices are under ground.
It was to have had a fine portico the whole range of
the building; but unluckily the governor and assembly disagreeing about ways and means, the execution of the design was suspended; and only the
shell of the house has been finished, which is now
going to ruin. The house which the present gov-

ernor inhabits, is hired by the province at 80 l. currency per annum.

There is very little trade carried on from this place, and the chief of the inhabitants are storekeepers or public officers. They build two or three ships annually, but seldom more. There are no fortifications, except a miserable battery of fifteen six-pounders.

Maryland is situated between the 38th and 40th degree of north latitude, and the 75th and 80th of west longitude from London. It is bounded on the east by the Atlantic ocean, and the three lower counties of Delaware; on the south and west by Virginia; and by Pennsylvania on the north. The climate, soil, and natural productions of it are nearly the same as those of Virginia. It is watered by many fine rivers, and almost innumerable creeks; but it is far from being well cultivated, and is capable of much improvement. It is divided into fourteen counties, and between forty and fifty parishes; and there are several little towns in it which are neatly built. The inhabitants, exclusive of slaves, are supposed to be about ninety thousand: of which the militia, including all white males between sixteen and fifty, amounts to eighteen. The slaves are about thirty-two thousand. The staple of the country is tobacco; and, *communibus annis*, they export near 30,000 hogsheads: last year their exports amounted to 50,000. Their manufactures are very trifling. The government is a proprietary one; and consists of the proprietor (viz. Lord Baltimore); his governor, the council, composed of twelve persons nominated by himself, and a house of representatives, elected by the people; four for each county, and two for Annapolis. The power of the proprietor is next to regal; of the other parts of the legislature, much the same as in Virginia. The lower house has been at variance some years with the council and governor, concerning ways and means; chiefly in regard to taxing the merchants' book-debts: which has been the reason of their having done nothing for the defence of the colonies during the war. The house has constantly voted troops, but as constantly laid the same tax for the maintenance of them: the council therefore has always rejected the bill; alleging the inconvenience of such a tax, as it would necessarily be a restraint upon trade; and ruin many of the merchants' credit. —The proprietor has a negative* upon every bill, exclusive of his governor.

There are several courts of judicature in this province, but the principal are either those which are held quarterly in each county by the justices thereof, like those in Virginia; or the provincial ones, which are held twice annually at Annapolis

* This power is doubted, though it has never yet been contested.

by judges appointed for that purpose.*   The court of chancery consists of the governor and council: and the dernier resort is to his majesty in council at home.

The established religion is that of the Church of England: but there are as many Roman Catholics as Protestants.   The clergy are liberally provided for; they have not, as in Virginia, a fixed quantity of tobacco; but so much per head, viz. 30 lb. weight for every titheable in their respective parishes. and some of them make more than 300 l. sterling per annum.   They are presented to their livings by the governor; and are under the jurisdiction of the bishop of London; but being at a great distance from England, and having no commissary to super-intend their affairs, they lie under many disadvan-tages.   Assessments are made, I was told, by the county courts; the vestry, which consists of twelve members distinct from the church wardens, have little or no authority †

In each county throughout this province, there is a public free school, for reading, writing, and accounts; but no college or academy; and the edu-cation of youth is but little attended to.

* Besides these courts, there was formerly a general court of assize held throughout the province either once or twice a year, but this has been laid aside

† The whole vestry, as in Virginia, consists of twelve members, but they go off by rotation two every year; and there is annually a fresh election.   They have the power of appointing inspectors, etc.

Chesapeake-Bay

The character of the inhabitants is much the same
as that of the Virginians; and the state of the two
colonies nearly alike. Tobacco, to speak in general,
is the chief thing attended to in both. There have
been some attempts to make wine; and it is certain,
that the country is capable of producing almost any
sort of grapes. Col. Tasco, a gentleman of distinction in these parts, attempted to make Burgundy,
and succeeded tolerably well for the first trial. I
drank some of the wine at the table of Mr. Hamilton,
the governor of Pennsylvania, and thought it not
bad. But whether, as this gentleman is now de-
ceased, any other person will have spirit to prosecute his plan, I much doubt. The currency here
is paper money, and the difference of exchange
about fifty per cent. The duty upon negroes is
only forty shillings currency per head at their importation; whereas in Virginia it is ten pounds.

June 13. I hired a schooner of about ten ton,
and embarked for the head of the bay, distant
twenty-three leagues; we made sail with a fresh
breeze, and after a pleasant passage of sixteen hours,
in one of the most delightful days imaginable, arrived at Fredericktown upon Sassafras river, about
twelve in the evening. I never in my life spent a
day more agreeably, or with higher entertainment.
The shores on each side of the bay, and the many
little islands interspersed in it, afford very beautiful
prospects; we were entertained at the same time by

innumerable porpoises playing about the bow of the ship; and naturally fell into a train of the most pleasing reflections, on observing the mouths of the many noble rivers as we passed along. On the western shore, besides those great rivers of Virginia, which I have already described, there are ten or eleven others, large and capacious, some of them navigable a considerable way up into the country.* "The Patuxent, which we have left behind us," said the master of the schooner, as we were sailing over this beautiful bay, "is navigable near fifty miles for vessels of three hundred ton burthen. Yonder," he added, "are South, Severn, and Magotty rivers, navigable about ten miles. A little farther is the Patapsico, a large and noble river; where I have gone up fifteen miles. Back, Middle, Gunpowder, and Bush rivers admit only sloops and schooners, and these only for six or seven miles. The Susquehanna, though so majestic, and superior in appearance, has only a short, and that a bad navigation; but it rises an immense way off in unknown and inhospitable regions, is exceedingly large and beautiful, and affords great variety of fish. The next, or North river, is navigable about ten miles. On the eastern shore," he concluded, "are Elk, Bahama, Sassafras, Chester, Wye, Miles, Great Choptank, Little Choptank, Nan-

* By some error or oversight the names of several rivers here mentioned, though particularly specified in the original manuscript, were omitted in the first and second editions of this work They are now inserted, and the account is correct.

ticote, Manokin, and Pocomoke rivers, all of them navigable, more or less, for several miles* " Such was our conversation and entertainment during this delightful voyage.

Frederictown is a small village on the western side of Sassafras river, built for the accommodation of strangers and travellers; on the eastern side, exactly opposite to it, is another small village (Georgetown), erected for the same purpose. Having hired an Italian chaise, with a servant and horse to attend me as far as Philadelphia, I left Frederictown the next day, and went to Newcastle, thirty-two miles.

Newcastle is situated upon Delaware river, about forty miles above the Bay, and a hundred from the Capes. It is the capital of the three lower counties, but a place of very little consideration; there are scarcely more than a hundred houses in it, and no public buildings that deserve to be taken notice of. The church, Presbyterian and Quaker meeting-houses, court-house, and market-house, are almost equally bad, and undeserving of attention.

The province, of which this is the capital, and which is distinguished by the name of the Three Lower Counties of Newcastle, Sussex, and Kent, belonged formerly to the Dutch; but was ratified to the crown of England by the treaty of Breda; it was afterwards sold by the Duke of York to the proprietor of Pennsylvania, and has continued a

* He said from eighteen to fifty miles.

separate government, though under nearly the same regulations with that province, ever since. The same governor presides over both; but the assembly, and courts of judicature are different: different as to their constituent members, for in form they are nearly alike. The assembly consists of eighteen persons, elected annually by the people; six for each county: this, with the governor, forms the legislature of the province. There is a militia, in which all persons, from eighteen to fifty, are obliged to be enrolled; and the county of Newcastle alone furnishes more than seven hundred.

The next day I set out for Philadelphia, distant about thirty-six miles, and arrived there in the evening. The country all the way bore a different aspect from any thing I had hitherto seen in America. It was much better cultivated, and beautifully laid out into fields of clover, grain, and flax. I passed by a very pretty village called Wilmington; and rode through two others, viz. Chester and Derby. The Delaware river is in sight great part of the way, and is three miles broad. Upon the whole nothing could be more pleasing than the ride which I had this day. I ferried over the Schuylkill, about three miles below Philadelphia; from whence to the city the whole country is covered with villas, gardens, and luxuriant orchards.

Philadelphia, if we consider that not eighty years ago the place where it now stands was a wild and uncultivated desert, inhabited by nothing but ravenous beasts, and a savage people, must certainly be the object of every one's wonder and admiration. It is situated upon a tongue of land, a few miles above the confluence of the Delaware and Schuylkill; and contains about 3,000 houses, and 18 or 20,000 inhabitants It is built north and south upon the banks of the Delaware; and is nearly two miles in length, and three quarters of one in breadth. The streets are laid out with great regularity in parallel lines, intersected by others at right angles, and are handsomely built· on each side there is a pavement of broad stones for foot passengers; and in most of them a causeway in the middle for carriages. Upon dark nights it is well lighted, and watched by a patrol: there are many fair houses, and public edifices in it. The stadt-house is a large, handsome, though heavy building; in this are held the councils, the assemblies, and supreme courts; there are apartments in it also for the accommodation of Indian chiefs or sachems; likewise two libraries, one belonging to the province, the other to a society, which was incorporated about ten years ago, and consists of sixty members. Each member upon admission, subscribed forty shillings; and afterward annually ten. They can alienate their shares, by will or deed, to any person approved by the society. They have a small collection of medals and medallions, and a few other curiosities, such as the skin of a rattle-snake killed at Surinam twelve feet long; and several Northern Indian habits made of furs and skins At a small distance from the stadt-house, there is another fine library, consisting of a very valuable and chosen collection of books, left by a Mr. Logan; they are chiefly in the learned languages.* Near this there is also a noble hospital for lunatics, and other sick persons. Besides these buildings, there are spacious barracks for 17 or 1800 men; a good assembly-room belonging to the society of Free Masons; and eight or ten places of religious worship; viz. two churches, three Quaker meeting-houses, two Presbyterian ditto, one Lutheran church, one Dutch Calvinist ditto, one Swedish ditto, one Romish chapel, one Anabaptist meeting-house, one Moravian ditto: there is also an academy or college, originally built for a tabernacle for Mr. Whitefield. At the south end of the town, upon the river, there is a battery mounting thirty guns, but it is in a state of decay. It was designed to be a check upon privateers. These, with a few alms-houses, and a school-house belonging to the Quakers, are the chief public buildings in Philadelphia. The city is in a very flourishing state, and inhabited by merchants, artists, tradesmen, and persons of all occupations. There is a public market held twice a week, upon Wednesday and Saturday, almost equal to that of Leadenhall, and a tolerable one every day besides.

* See Note IX.

Philadelphia

The streets are crowded with people, and the river with vessels. Houses are so dear, that they will let for 100 l. currency per annum; and lots, not above thirty feet in breadth, and a hundred in length, in advantageous situations, will sell for 1,000 l. sterling. There are several docks upon the river, and about twenty-five vessels are built there annually. I counted upon the stocks at one time no less than seventeen, many of them three-masted vessels.*

Can the mind have a greater pleasure than in contemplating the rise and progress of cities and kingdoms? Than in perceiving a rich and opulent state arising out of a small settlement or colony? This pleasure every one must feel who considers Pensylvania. This wonderful province is situated between the 40th and 43d degree of north latitude, and about 76 degrees west longitude from London, in a healthy and delightful climate, amidst all the advantages that nature can bestow. The soil is extremely strong and fertile, and produces spontaneously an infinite variety of trees, flowers, fruits, and plants of different sorts. The mountains are enriched with ore, and the rivers with fish: some of these are so stately as not to be beheld without admiration: the Delaware is navigable for large vessels as far as the falls, 180 miles distant from the sea, and 120 from the bay. At the mouth it is more than three miles broad, and above one at Philadelphia.

* See Appendix, No. 2.

The navigation is obstructed in the winter, for about six weeks, by the severity of the frost; but, at other times, it is bold and open. The Schuylkill, though not navigable for any great space, is exceedingly romantic, and affords the most delightful retirements.

Cultivation (comparatively speaking) is carried to a high degree of perfection; and Pennsylvania produces not only great plenty, but also great variety of grain; it yields likewise flax-seed, hemp, cattle of different kinds, and various other articles.*

It is divided into eight counties, and contains many large and populous towns: Carlisle, Lancaster, and Germantown, consist each of near five hundred houses; there are several others which have from one or two hundred.

The number of inhabitants is supposed to be between four and five hundred thousand,† a fifth of

* In the southern colonies cultivation is in a very low state The common process of it is, first to cut off the trees two or three feet above ground, in order to let in the sun and air, leaving the stumps to decay and rot, which they do in a few years After this they dig and plant, and continue to work the same field, year after year, without ever manuring it, till it is quite spent. They then enter upon a fresh piece of ground, allowing this a respite of about twenty years to recover itself, during which time it becomes beautifully covered with Virginian pines; the seeds of that tree, which are exceedingly small, and, when the cones open, are wafted through the air in great abundance, sowing themselves in every vacant spot of neglected ground.

† Doubts have since arisen, whether the number, at the time here mentioned, amounted to more than 350,000.—See Morse's American Geography.

which are Quakers; there are very few negroes or slaves.

The trade of Pennsylvania is surprisingly extensive, carried on to Great Britain, the West Indies, every part of North America, the Madeiras, Lisbon, Cadiz, Holland, Africa, the Spanish Main, and several other places; exclusive of what is illicitly carried on to Cape François, and Monte Christo. Their exports are provisions of all kinds, lumber, hemp, flax, flax-seed, iron, furs, and deer-skins Their imports, English manufactures, with the superfluities and luxuries of life. By their flag-of-truce trade, they also get sugar, which they refine and send to Europe.

Their manufactures are very considerable. The Germantown thread-stockings are in high estimation; and the year before last, I have been credibly informed, there were manufactured in that town alone above 60,000 dozen pair. Their common retail price is a dollar per pair.

The Irish settlers make very good linens: some woolens have also been fabricated, but not, I believe, to any amount. There are several other manufactures, viz. of beaver hats, which are superior in goodness to any in Europe, of cordage, linseed-oil, starch, myrtle-wax and spermaceti candles, soap, earthen ware, and other commodities.

The government of this province is a proprietary one. The legislature is lodged in the hands of a governor, appointed (with the king's approbation) by the proprietor; and a house of representatives elected by the people, consisting of thirty-seven members. These are of various religious persuasions; for by the charter of privileges which Mr. Penn granted to the settlers in Pennsylvania, no person who believed in God could be molested in his calling or profession; and any one who believed in Jesus Christ might enjoy the first post under the government. The crown has reserved to itself a power of repealing any law, which may interfere with the prerogative, or be contrary to the laws of Great Britain.

The judicature consists of different courts. The justices of the peace, who, together with the other judges, are of the governor's appointments, hold quarterly sessions conformable to the laws of England; and, when these are finished, continue to sit in quality of judges of common pleas, by a special commission. The supreme court consists of a chief justice, and two assistant judges; they have the united authority of the King's Bench, Common Pleas, and Court of Exchequer. They not only receive appeals, but all causes once commenced in the inferior courts, after the first writ, may be moved thither by a habeas corpus, certiorari, writ of error, etc. The judges of the supreme court have also a standing and distinct commission, to hold, as shall seem needful, courts of oyer and terminer, and general gaol-deliveries throughout the province; but this power they seldom, I believe, exercise. The supreme courts are held twice a year at Philadelphia. There is no Court of Chancery; but the want of it is supplied, in some measure, by the other courts. There is a particular officer called the register-general, appointed by the governor, whose authority extends over the whole province, where he has several deputies. He grants letters of administration, and probates of wills. In cases of dispute, or caveat entered, he may call in, as assistants, two justices of the peace. The governor can pardon in all cases, except of treason or murder, and then can reprieve till he knows the king's pleasure.

There is here, as in most of the other colonies, a Court of Vice-Admiralty, held by commission from the Admiralty in England, for the trial of captures, and of piracies, and other misdemeanors committed upon the high seas; but there lies an appeal from it, I believe, to the Court of Delegates in England.

As to religion, there is none properly established, but Protestants of all denominations, Papists, Jews, and all other sects whatsoever, are universally tolerated. There are twelve clergymen of the Church of England, who are sent by the Society for the Propagation of the Gospel, and are allowed annually 50 l. each, besides what they get from subscriptions and surplice fees. Some few of these are itinerant missionaries, and have no fixed residence, but travel from place to place, as occasion requires, upon the frontiers. They are under the jurisdiction of the bishop of London.

Arts and sciences are yet in their infancy. There are some few persons who have discovered a taste for music and painting*; and philosophy seems not only to have made a considerable progress already, but to be daily gaining ground. The library society is an excellent institution for propagating a taste for literature; and the college well calculated to form and cultivate it. This last institution is erected upon an admirable plan, and is by far the best school for learning throughout America. It has been chiefly raised by contributions; and its present fund is about 10,000 l. Pennsylvania money. An account of it may be seen in Dr. Smith's (the president's) Discourses. The Quakers also have an academy for instructing their youth in classical learning, and practical mathematics: there are three teachers, and about seventy boys in it. Besides these, there are several schools in the province for the Dutch and other foreign children; and a considerable one is going to be erected at Germantown.

The Pennsylvanians, as to character, are a frugal and industrious people: not remarkably courteous and hospitable to strangers, unless particularly recommended to them; but rather, like the denizens of most commercial cities, the reverse. They are

* Mr. Benjamin West, president of the Royal Academy, was, I believe, a native of Pennsylvania, if not of Philadelphia.

great republicans, and have fallen into the same errors in their ideas of independency as most of the other colonies have. They are by far the most enterprising people upon the continent. As they consist of several nations, and talk several languages, they are aliens in some respect to Great Britain: nor can it be expected that they should have the same filial attachment to her which her own immediate offspring have. However, they are quiet, and concern themselves but little, except about getting money. The women are exceedingly handsome and polite; they are naturally sprightly and fond of pleasure; and, upon the whole, are much more agreeable and accomplished than the men. Since their intercourse with the English officers, they are greatly improved; and, without flattery, many of them would not make bad figures even in the first assemblies in Europe. Their amusements are chiefly, dancing in the winter; and, in the summer, forming parties of pleasure upon the Schuylkill, and in the country. There is a society of sixteen ladies, and as many gentlemen, called the fishing company, who meet once a fortnight upon the Schuylkill. They have a very pleasant room erected in a romantic situation upon the banks of that river, where they generally dine and drink tea. There are several pretty walks about it, and some wild and rugged rocks, which, together with the water and fine groves that adorn the banks, form a most beautiful and

picturesque scene. There are boats and fishing
tackle of all sorts, and the company divert themselves with walking, fishing, going up the water,
dancing, singing, conversing, or just as they please.
The ladies wear an uniform, and appear with great
ease and advantage from the neatness and simplicity of it. The first and most distinguished people
of the colony are of this society; and it is very advantageous to a stranger to be introduced to it, as
he hereby gets acquainted with the best and most
respectable company in Philadelphia. In the winter,
when there is snow upon the ground, it is usual to
make what they call sleighing parties, or to go upon
it in sledges; but as this is a practice well known in
Europe, it is needless to describe it.

The present state of Pennsylvania is undoubtedly
very flourishing. The country is well cultivated,
and there are not less than 9,000 wagons employed
in it, in different services. Till this war they were
exempt from taxes; and it was not without difficulty
that the Quakers were prevailed upon to grant any
supplies for the defence of the frontiers, though exposed to the most horrid cruelties: it was not from
principle, say their enemies, that they refused it,
but from interest; for as they were the first settlers,
they chiefly occupy the interior and lower parts of
the province, and are not exposed to incursions.
At length, however, compelled by clamour and public discontent, they were obliged to pass a supply

bill for 100,000 l. to raise five and twenty hundred men; and these they have kept up ever since; they afterward passed a militia bill, but it was such an one as answered no good purpose. The Quakers have much the greatest influence in the assembly, and are supported there by the Dutch and Germans, who are as adverse to taxes as themselves. Their power, however, at present seems rather on the decline; which is the reason, as the opposite party pretend, that they stir upon all occasions as much confusion as possible, from that trite maxim in politics, *divide et impera.* They have quarrelled with the proprietors upon several occasions, whether altogether justly or not, I will not pretend to say; it is certain, however, that the determinations at home have been sometimes in their favour. The late subjects of their disputes have been chiefly these:

First, Whether the proprietary lands ought to be taxed? This has been determined at home in the affirmative.

Secondly, Whether the proprietor ought to have any choice or approbation of the assessors?

Thirdly, Whether he ought to give his governor instructions? And,

Lastly, Whether the judges of his appointment ought to be during pleasure, or *quamdiu se bene gesserint?* These three last are still undecided.

Upon the whole, though this province is exceedingly flourishing, yet there are certainly great abuses in it; and such as, if not speedily rectified, will be productive of bad consequences.

The difference of exchange between bills and the currency of Pennsylvania, is about 75 per cent.

An occurrence happened to me at Philadelphia, which, though in itself of a trifling nature, I cannot but take notice of, as a singular instance of the strong possession which an idea will sometimes take of the mind; so as totally to derange it. A lady from Rhode Island, who lodged in the same house with myself, had an unfortunate brother in the infirmary, a lunatic. He was supposed to be nearly well, and was permitted occasionally to see company. A few days before I was to leave Philadelphia, this lady invited me to accompany her in one of her visits to him; adding, that on her inadvertently mentioning to him some circumstances relating to me, he had expressed a most earnest desire to see me. I strongly objected to the proposal, urging the impropriety of introducing a stranger, or, indeed, company of any sort, to a person in that unhappy situation; as it might possibly agitate his mind, and retard his recovery. I advised her therefore not to take any further notice of it; hoping he might forget, or not mention it any more. The next day she renewed her application, adding, that her brother was exceedingly disappointed; and entreated me to attend her, in so pressing a manner, that I could not with civility refuse it. On entering the cell, a beam of

satisfaction seemed to dart from his eye, not easy to
be expressed or conceived. I took him by the hand;
and, seating myself opposite the bed to which he was
chained, immediately took the lead in conversation,
talking of indifferent matters, such as I thought
could not possibly tend to interest or disturb his
mind. I had not proceeded far when he suddenly
interrupted me; and proposed a question, which at
once convinced me that he was in a very unfit state
to see company. I immediately therefore rose up;
and making an excuse that my engagements that
day would not admit of my entering into so curious
a subject, desired him to reserve it for some future
conversation. He seemed greatly disconcerted; but
being near the door, which stood open, I took my
leave and retired. The next morning I left Philadelphia; nor did I think any more of this occurrence
till I arrived at Rhode Island, where I was informed
that the chief, if not sole, instances of insanity
shewn by this unhappy young man, were some attempts which he had made to kill a clergyman of
the Church of England. That he had been educated to be a teacher amongst the Congregationalists,
but had taken it into his head that he could never
gain heaven, or be happy, but by committing so
heroic and meritorious an action. The very evening of his confinement he was prevented from ful-
filling his purpose, in the instant when he was raising
up his hand to plunge a knife into the back of a

clergyman, who was reading the funeral service, in the presence of a large congregation. What his intentions were in regard to myself, I cannot pretend to say; he offered me no violence: but those at Rhode Island of his acquaintance, to whom I related this transaction, were fully persuaded that he was far from being cured of his distemper *

I left Philadelphia the 6th of July, and travelled

* Since my return to Europe, I have been informed of an instance similar to this, which happened at Florence. A gentleman had taken it into his head that a very large diamond lay buried under a mountain which stood upon his estate, and was near ruining himself and his family by digging for it His friends, by some contrivance or other, got him away to Florence, and placed him under the care of the late celebrated Dr. Cocchi He there appeared perfectly composed, talked very rationally, and, having been well educated, afforded great entertainment to the doctor and his friends, who conversed with him One day as they were sitting together, he mentioned to the doctor, that it was very hard he should be deprived of his liberty, when he was perfectly well, and that it was only a scheme of his relations to keep him in confinement, in order that they might enjoy his estate. The doctor, who had perceived no marks of insanity, began to be staggered; and promised, in case he should see no reason to alter his sentiments, to sign a certificate of his being well on such a day, in order to its being sent to England, that he might have his release The day arrived, and the doctor was preparing to perform his promise, but, whether by design on perceiving something particular in the looks of his patient, or by accident, I could not learn, he said to the gentleman "Now, Sir, I beg from this time that you will think no "more of this foolish affair of the mountain and diamond." "Not "think of the diamond," said the madman, "it is for this reason "that I want my liberty, I know exactly the spot where it lies; and "I will have it in my possession, before I am a year older"
This story was related to me in Tuscany, and I had no reason to question the truth of it.

in the stage as far as Sheminey-ferry, about seventeen miles; where I was overtaken by a gentleman and some ladies of my acquaintance, who were going a few miles farther upon a party of pleasure. They were so obliging as to make room for me in one of their chaises, and we proceeded and dined together at Bristol, a small town upon the Delaware, opposite Burlington: in the afternoon we went ten miles higher up the river, and ferried over to Trenton, situated in the Jerseys. This is built on the east side of the Delaware, and contains about a hundred houses. It has nothing remarkable; there is a church, a Quaker and Presbyterian meeting-house, and barracks for three hundred men. From hence we went to Sir John Sinclair's, at the Falls of Delaware, about a mile above Trenton, a pleasant rural retirement, where we spent a most agreeable evening. In the morning, the company returned to Philadelphia; and, having hired a chaise, I proceeded to Princeton, twelve miles distant.

At this place, there is a handsome school and college for the education of dissenters, erected upon the plan of those in Scotland. There are about twenty boys in the grammar-school, and sixty in the college: at present there are only two professors, besides the provost; but they intend, as their fund increases, which is yet very small, and does not exceed 2,000 l. currency, to add to this number. The building is extremely convenient, airy, and spacious;

and has a chapel and other proper offices. Two students are in each set of apartments, which consists of a large bed-room with a fire-place, and two studies. There is a small collection of books, a few instruments, and some natural curiosities. The expense to a student for room-rent, commons, and tutorage, amounts to 25 l. currency per year. The provost has a salary of 200 l. currency, and the professors 50 l. each. The name of the college is Nassau Hall. From hence, in the afternoon, I proceeded to Brunswick, eighteen miles farther, a small town of about a hundred houses, situated upon Raritan river, where there are also very neat barracks for 300 men, a church, and a Presbyterian meeting-house. It is celebrated for the number of its beauties; and, indeed, at this place and Philadelphia, were the handsomest women that I saw in America. At a small distance from the town is a copper-mine belonging to a Mr. French, (I was told) a pretty good one. The next day I rode up the river, about nine miles to the Raritan hills, to see a small cascade, which falls about fifteen or twenty feet, very romanticly, from between two rocks. The country I passed through is exceedingly rich and beautiful; and the banks of the river are covered with gentlemen's houses. At one of these I had an opportunity of seeing some good portraits of Vandyck, and several other small Dutch paintings.

On Monday the 7th, I proceeded to Perth Amboy,

twelve miles, the capital of the East Jerseys, which is pleasantly situated upon a neck of land, included between the Raritan and Amboy rivers and a large open bay. This is generally the place of the governor's residence; and alternately, here and at Burlington, the capital of the West Jerseys, are held the assemblies, and other public meetings; it contains about a hundred houses, and has very fine barracks for 300 men. In the afternoon I travelled sixteen miles farther to Elizabethtown, leaving Woodbridge, a small village where there is a printing-office, a little on my right hand. Elizabethtown is built upon a small creek or river that falls into Newark bay, and contains between two and three hundred houses. It has a court-house, a church, and a meeting-house; and barracks also like those above mentioned.

The next morning I rode out, in order to visit Passaic Falls, distant about twenty-three miles, and had a very agreeable tour. After riding six miles I came to a town called Newark, built in an irregular scattered manner, after the fashion of some of our villages in England, near two miles in length. It has a church erected in the Gothic taste with a spire, the first I had seen in America, and some other inconsiderable public buildings. Immediately on my leaving this place, I came upon the banks of Second, or Passaic river, along which I travelled seventeen or eighteen miles to the Falls, through a

rich country, interspersed with fine fields and gentlemen's seats.

The Falls are very extraordinary, different from
any I had hitherto met with in America. The river
is about forty yards broad, and runs with a very
swift current, till coming to a deep chasm or cleft,
which crosses the channel, it falls above seventy feet
perpendicular in one entire sheet. One end of the
cleft is closed up, and the water rushes out at the
other with incredible rapidity, in an acute angle to
its former direction; and is received into a large
basin. Hence it takes a winding course through
the rocks, and spreads again into a very considerable channel. The cleft is from four to twelve feet
broad. The spray formed two beautiful (viz. the
primary and secondary) rainbows, and helped to
make as fine a scene as imagination could conceive.
This extraordinary phenomenon is supposed to have
been produced by an earthquake The fate of two
Indians is delivered down by tradition, who, ven-
turing too near the Falls in a canoe, were carried
down the precipice, and dashed to pieces, Thirty
or forty yards above the great Fall, is another, a
most beautiful one, gliding over some ledges of rocks
each two or three feet perpendicular, which heightens
the scene very much.

From hence I returned, and in my way crossed
over the river to Colonel John Schuyler's copper

mines, where there is a very rich vein of ore, and a fire-engine erected upon common principles.

After this I went down two miles farther to the park and gardens of this gentleman's brother, Colonel Peter Schuyler. In the gardens is a very large collection of citrons, oranges, limes, lemons, balsams of Peru, aloes, pomegranates, and other tropical plants; and in the park I saw several American and English deer, and three or four elks or moose-deer I arrived at Elizabethtown in the evening, not a little entertained with my expedition, but exceedingly fatigued with the violent heat of the weather and the many mosquitoes that had infested me.

Before I take leave of the Jerseys, it is necessary I should give some account of this province. New Jersey is situated between the 39th and 42d degree of north latitude, and about seventy-five degrees west longitude: it is bounded on the east by the Atlantic, on the west by Pennsylvania, or to speak more properly the Delaware; on the south by Delaware bay; and on the north by Hudson's river and the province of New York, The climate is nearly the same as that of Pennsylvania· and the soil, which is a kind of red slate, is so exceedingly rich, that in a short time after it has been turned up and exposed to the air and moisture, it is converted into a species of marl.*

* Since my return from America, I have met with a gentleman (Edward Wortley Montagu, Esq) who had visited the Holy Land.

New Jersey has very great natural advantages of hills, valleys, rivers, and large bays. The Delaware is on one side, and Hudson's river on the other; besides which it has the Raritan, Passaic, and Amboy rivers; and Newark and New York bays. It produces vast quantities of grain, besides hemp, flax, hay, Indian corn, and other articles. It is divided into eleven counties, and has several small towns, though not one of consideration. The number of its inhabitants is supposed to be 70,000: of which, all males between sixteen and sixty, negroes excepted, are obliged to serve in the militia. There is no foreign trade carried on from this province; for the inhabitants sell their produce to the merchants of Philadelphia and New York, and take in return European goods and other necessaries of life. They have some trifling manufactures of their own, but nothing that deserves mentioning.

The government consists of a governor, twelve counsellors, and a house of representatives of about twenty-six members, the two former nominated by the king, the latter elected by the people. Each branch has a negative; they meet at Amboy and at Burlington alternately. The governor's salary, with

He described the soil of that country to be similar in almost every circumstance to this of the Jerseys. He said it appeared to be of a red slaty substance, sterile, and incapable of producing any thing worth the cultivation; but that being broken up and exposed to the air, it became exceedingly mellow, and was fertile in the highest degree.

perquisites, is about 800, or 1,000 l. sterling a year; he is not allowed a house to reside in, but is obliged to hire one at his own expense. There are several courts of judicature here, much like those of the other provinces. The justices hold quarterly sessions for petty larcenies, and trifling causes: and the supreme judge, with two assistant justices, holds, once a year, a general assize, throughout the province, of oyer and terminer, and common pleas. He holds also annually four supreme courts, alternately at Amboy and Burlington, of king's-bench, common-pleas, and exchequer. The offices of chancellor and vice-admiral, are executed by the governor; and the dernier resort is to his majesty in council.

There is properly no established religion in this province, and the inhabitants are of various persuasions: the society sends six missionaries, who are generally well received; and the church gains ground daily. Their salaries are about the same as in Pennsylvania.

Arts and sciences are here, as in the other parts of America, just dawning. The college will in time, without doubt, be of considerable advantage, but being yet in its infancy, it has not had an opportunity of operating, or effecting any visible improvement.

The New Jersey men, as to character, are like most country gentlemen, good natured, hospitable, and of a more liberal turn than their neighbours the

Pennsylvanians. They live altogether upon their estates, and are literally gentlemen farmers. The country in its present state can scarcely be called flourishing; for although it is extremely well cultivated, thickly seated, and the garden of North America, yet, having no foreign trade, it is deprived of those riches and advantages, which it would otherwise soon acquire. There have been some attempts to remedy this defect; but whether from the difficulty of diverting a thing out of a channel in which it has long flowed; or from want of propriety or perseverance, in the measures, I am unable to say; but the truth is, they have not succeeded. Upon the whole, however, this province may be called a rich one: during the present war it has raised considerable supplies, having seldom had less than 1,000 men in pay, with a leader (Colonel Schuyler) at their head, who has done honour to his country by his patriotic and public spirit. The paper currency of this colony is at about 70 per cent. discount, but in very good repute; and preferred by the Pennsylvanians and New Yorkers to that of their own provinces.

On Wednesday the 9th of July, I crossed over to Staten Island, in the province of New York; and travelled upon it about nine miles to the point which is opposite New York City.

In my way I had an opportunity of seeing the method of making wampum. This, the reader probably knows is the current money amongst the

Indians. It is made of the clam shell; a shell, consisting within of two colours, purple and white; and in form not unlike a thick oyster shell. The process of manufacturing it is very simple. It is first clipped to a proper size, which is that of a small oblong parallelopiped, then drilled, and afterward ground to a round smooth surface, and polished. The purple wampum is much more valuable than the white, a very small part of the shell being of that colour.

At the point I embarked for New York; and, after a pleasant passage over the bay, which is three leagues wide; and various delightful prospects of rivers, islands, fields, hills, woods, the Narrows, New York City, vessels sailing to and fro, and innumerable porpoises playing upon the surface of the water, in an evening so serene that the hemisphere was not ruffled by a single cloud, arrived there about the setting of the sun.

This city is situated upon the point of a small island, lying open to the bay on one side, and on the others included between the North and East rivers; and commands a fine prospect of water, the Jerseys, Long Island, Staten Island, and several others, which lie scattered in the bay. It contains between two and three thousand houses, and 16 or 17,000 inhabitants, is tolerably well built, and has several good houses. The streets are paved, and very clean, but in general narrow; there are two or three, indeed, which are spacious and airy, particularly the Broadway. The houses in this street have most of them a row of trees before them; which form an agreeable shade, and produce a pretty effect. The whole length of the town is something more than a mile; the breadth of it about half an one. The situation is, I believe, esteemed healthy; but it is subject to one great inconvenience, which is the want of fresh water; so that the inhabitants are obliged to have it brought from springs at some distance out of town. There are several public buildings, though but few that deserve attention. The college, when finished, will be exceedingly handsome; it is to be built on three sides of a quadrangle, fronting Hudson's or North river, and will be the most beautifully situated of any college, I believe, in the world. At present only one wing is finished, which is of stone, and consists of twenty-four sets of apartments; each having a large sitting-room, with a study, and bed-chamber. They are obliged to make use of some of these apartments for a master's lodge, library, chapel, hall, etc., but as soon as the whole shall be completed, there will be proper apartments for each of these offices. The name of it is King's College.

There are two churches in New York, the old or Trinity Church, and the new one, or St. George's Chapel;* both of them large buildings, the former

* See Note X.

in the Gothic taste, with a spire, the other upon the model of some of the new churches in London. Besides these, there are several other places of religious worship; namely, two Low Dutch Calvinist churches, one High Dutch ditto, one French ditto, one German Lutheran church, one Presbyterian meeting-house, one Quaker ditto, one Anabaptists ditto, one Moravian ditto, and a Jews synagogue. There is also a very handsome charity-school for sixty poor boys and girls, a good work-house, barracks for a regiment of soldiers, and one of the finest prisons I have ever seen.* The court or stadt-house makes no great figure, but it is to be repaired and beautified. There is a quadrangular fort,† capable of mounting sixty cannon, though at present there are, I believe, only thirty-two. Within this is the governor's palace, and underneath it a battery capable of mounting ninety-four guns, and barracks for a company or two of soldiers. Upon one of the islands in the bay is an hospital for sick and wounded seamen; and, upon another, a pest-house. These are the most noted public buildings in and about the city.

The province of New York is situated between the 40th and 45th degree of north latitude, and about 75 degrees west longitude. It lies in a fine climate, and enjoys a very wholesome air. The soil of most

* See Note XI.

† See Note XII.

parts of it is extremely good, particularly of Long Island· and it has the advantages of a fine harbour, and fine rivers. The bay has a communication with Newark bay, the Sound, Amboy river, and several others: it receives also Hudson's or North river, one of the largest in North America, it being navigable for sloops as far as Albany, above 150 miles: whence, by the Mohawk, and other rivers, running through the country of the Six Nations, there is a communication, (excepting a few short carrying places,) with lake Ontario; and another with the river St. Laurence, through the lakes George, Champlain, and the river Sorel; so that this river seems to merit the greatest attention. These waters afford various kinds of fish, black-fish, sea-bass, sheeps-heads, rock-fish, lobsters, and several others, all excellent in their kind. The province in its cultivated state affords grain of all sorts, cattle, hogs, and great variety of English fruits, particularly the Newtown pippin. It is divided into ten counties, and has some few towns, but none of any size, except Albany and Schenectady, the former of which is a very considerable place. The number of inhabitants amounts to nearly 100,000; 15 or 20,000 of which are supposed to be capable of bearing arms, and of serving in the militia; but I believe this number is exaggerated, as a considerable part of the 100,000 are negroes, which are imported more frequently into this province than into Pennsylvania. The people carry on an extensive trade, and there are said to be cleared out annually from New York,* tons of shipping. They export chiefly grain, flour, pork, skins, furs, pig iron, lumber, and staves. Their manufactures, indeed, are not extensive, nor by any means to be compared with those of Pennsylvania; they make a small quantity of cloth, some linen, hats, shoes, and other articles for wearing apparel. They make glass also, and wampum; refine sugars, which they import from the West Indies; and distill considerable quantities of rum. They also, as well as the Pennsylvanians, till both were restrained by act of Parliament, had erected several slitting mills, to make nails, etc. But this is now prohibited, and they are exceedingly dissatisfied at it. They have several other branches of manufactures, but, in general, so inconsiderable, that I shall not take notice of them: one thing it may be necessary to mention, I mean the article of shipbuilding; about which, in different parts of the province, they employ many hands.†

The government of this colony is lodged in the hands of a governor appointed by the crown; a council consisting of twelve members, named by the same authority; and a house of twenty-seven representatives, elected by the people: four for the city and county of New York, two for the city and county

* See Appendix, No. 2.

† See Appendix, No. 2.

of Albany; two for each of the other eight counties; one for the borough of West Chester; one for the township of Schenectady; and one for each of the three manors of Rensselaerwyck, Livingston, and Coitlandt. The legislative power is entirely lodged in their hands, each branch having a negative; except that, as in the other colonies, all laws must have the king's approbation, and not interfere with, or be repugnant to, the laws of Great Britain.

The courts of judicature are similar, I believe, in every respect, to those in the Jerseys.

The established religion is that of the Church of England, there being six churches in this province with stipends (to the value of about 50 l. currency) annexed to each by law. The clergy are twelve in number, who, exclusive of what they acquire by the establishment above-mentioned, or by contributions, receive, as missionaries from the Society for the Propagation of the Gospel, 50 l. sterling each. Besides the religion of the Church of England, there is a variety of others: dissenters of all denominations, particularly Presbyterians, abound in great numbers, and there are some few Roman Catholics.

Arts and sciences have made no greater progress here than in the other colonies; but as a subscription library* has been lately opened, and every one seems zealous to promote learning, it may be hoped they will hereafter advance faster than they have done

* See Note XIII.

hitherto. The college is established upon the same plan as that in the Jerseys, except that this at New York professes the principles of the Church of England. At present the state of it is far from being flourishing, or so good as might be wished. Its fund does not exceed 10,000 l. currency, and there is a great scarcity of professors. A commencement was held, nevertheless, this summer, and seven gentlemen took degrees. There are in it at this time about twenty-five students.* The president, Dr. Johnson, is a very worthy and learned man, but rather too far advanced in life to have the direction of so new an institution. The late Dr. Bristow left to this college a fine library, of which they are in daily expectation.

The inhabitants of New York, in their character, very much resemble the Pennsylvanians: more than half of them are Dutch, and almost all traders: they are, therefore, habitually frugal, industrious, and parsimonious. Being, however, of different nations, different languages, and different religions, it is almost impossible to give them any precise or determinate character. The women are handsome and agreeable; though rather more reserved than the Philadelphian ladies. Their amusements are much the same as in Pennsylvania; viz. balls, and sleighing expeditions in the winter; and, in the summer, going in parties upon the water, and fishing; or making

* See Note XIV.

excursions into the country. There are several
houses pleasantly situated upon East river, near New
York, where it is common to have turtle feasts: these
happen once or twice in a week. Thirty or forty
gentlemen and ladies meet and dine together, drink
tea in the afternoon, fish and amuse themselves till
evening, and then return home in Italian chaises,
(the fashionable carriage in this and most parts of
America, Virginia excepted, where they chiefly
make use of coaches, and these commonly drawn
by six horses), a gentleman and lady in each chaise.
In the way there is a bridge, about three miles distant from New York, which you always pass over
as you return, called the Kissing Bridge; where it
is a part of the etiquette to salute the lady who has
put herself under your protection.*

The present state of this province is flourishing:
it has an extensive trade to many parts of the world,
particularly to the West Indies; and has acquired
great riches by the commerce which it has carried
on, under flags of truce, to Cape François, and
Monte Christo. The troops, by having made it the
place of their general rendezvous, have also enriched
it very much. However, it is burthened with taxes,
and the present public debt amounts to more than
300,000 l. currency. The taxes are laid upon estates
real and personal; and there are duties upon negroes,
and other importations. The provincial troops are

* See Note XV.

about 2,600 men. The difference of exchange between currency and bills, is from 70 to 80 per cent.

Before I left New York, I took a ride upon Long Island, the richest spot, in the opinion of the New Yorkers, of all America; and where they generally have their villas, or country houses. It is undeniably beautiful, and some parts of it are remarkably fertile, but not equal, I think, to the Jerseys. The length of it is something more than 100 miles, and the breadth 25. About 15 or 16 miles from the west end of it, there opens a large plain between 20 and 30 miles long, and 4 or 5 broad. There is not a tree growing upon it, and it is asserted that there never were any. Strangers are always carried to see this place, as a great curiosity, and the only one of the kind in North America.

Tuesday, the 5th of August, being indisposed, and unable to travel any farther by land, I embarked on board a brigantine for Rhode Island. We made sail up the Sound with a fair wind, and after two hours, passed through Hell Gate. It is impossible to go through this place without recalling to mind the description of Scylla and Charybdis. The breadth of the Sound is here half a mile, but the channel is very narrow, not exceeding eighty yards: the water runs with great rapidity, and in different currents, only one of which will carry a vessel through with safety; for, on one side, there is a shoal of rocks just peeping above the water; and, on the other, a dreadful vortex produced by a rock lying about nine feet under the surface: if therefore you get into any but the right current, you are either dashed upon the shoal, or else sucked into the eddy, whirled round with incredible rapidity, and at length swallowed up in the vortex. There are exceeding good pilots to navigate vessels through this place, notwithstanding which, they are frequently lost. The proper time of passing it is at high water. We had pleasant weather during the passage, which is about seventy leagues, with beautiful views of Long Island and Connecticut; and arrived in the harbour at Newport the 7th of August.

This town is situated upon a small island, about twelve miles in length, and five or six in breadth, called Rhode Island, whence the province takes its name. It is the capital city, and contains 800, or 1,000 houses, chiefly built of wood; and 6 or 7000 inhabitants. There are few buildings in it worth notice. The courthouse is indeed handsome, and of brick; and there is a public library, built in the form of a Grecian temple, by no means inelegant.* It is of the Doric order, and has a portico in front with four pillars, supporting a pediment; but the whole is spoilt by two small wings, which are annexed to it. The foundation of a very pretty building is laid for the use of the Free Masons, to serve also occasionally for an assembly-room; and there is

* See XVI.

going to be erected a market-house, upon a very elegant design. The places of public worship, except the Jews' synagogue, are all of wood; and not one of them is worth looking at. They consist chiefly of a church, two Presbyterian meeting-houses, one Quaker ditto, three Anabaptists ditto, one Moravian ditto, and the synagogue above mentioned. This building was designed, as indeed were several of the others, by a Mr. Harrison, an ingenious English gentleman who lives here. It will be extremely elegant within when completed: but the outside is totally spoilt by a school, which the Jews would have annexed to it for the education of their children. Upon a small island, before the town, is part of a fine fortification, designed to consist of a pentagon fort, and an upper and lower battery. Only two of the curtains, and a ravelin, are yet finished; and it is doubted whether the whole will ever be completed. There are now mounted upon it 26 cannon; but the works, when complete, will require above 150. At the entrance of the harbour there is likewise an exceeding good light-house. These are the chief public buildings.

Three miles from the town is an indifferent wooden house, built by Dean Berkeley,* when he was in these parts: the situation is low, but commands a fine view of the ocean, and of some wild rugged rocks that are on the left hand of it. They relate here several

* See Note XVII.

stories of the dean's wild and chimerical notions; which, as they are characteristic of that extraordinary man, deserve to be taken notice of: one in particular I must beg the reader's indulgence to allow me to repeat to him. The dean had formed the plan of building a town upon the rocks which I have just now taken notice of, and of cutting a road through a sandy beach which lies a little below it, in order that ships might come up and be sheltered in bad weather. He was so full of this project, as one day to say to one Smibert, a designer,* whom he had brought over with him from Europe, on the latter's asking some ludicrous question concerning the future importance of the place: "Truly, you have very "little foresight, for in fifty years time every foot of "land in this place will be as valuable as the land in "Cheapside." The dean's house, notwithstanding his prediction, is at present nothing better than a farmhouse, and his library is converted into the dairy: when he left America, he gave it to the college at New Haven in Connecticut, who have let it to a farmer on a long lease: his books he divided between this college and that in Massachusetts. The dean is said to have written in this place The Minute Philosopher.

The province of Rhode Island is situated between the 41st and 42d degree of north latitude; and about 72 or 73 degrees west longitude, in the most healthy

* See Note XVIII.

climate of North America. The winters are severe, though not equally so with those of the other provinces; but the summers are delightful, especially in the island; the violent and excessive heats, to which America is in general subject, being allayed by the cool and temperate breezes that come from the sea. The soil is tolerably good, though rather too stony; its natural produce is maize or Indian corn, with a variety of shrubs and trees. It produces in particular the button-tree*; the spruce-pine, of the young twigs of which is made excellent beer; and the pseudo-acacia, or locust-tree; but none of those fine flowering trees, which are such an ornament to the woods in Carolina and Virginia. It enjoys many advantages, has several large rivers, and one of the finest harbours in the world. Fish are in the greatest plenty and perfection, particularly the tataag or black-fish, lobsters, and sea bass. In its cultivated state, it produces very little, except sheep and horned cattle, the whole province being laid out into pasture or grazing ground. The horses are bony and strong, and the oxen much the largest in America, several of them weighing from 16 to 1,800 weight. The butter and cheese are excellent.

The province of Rhode Island is divided into counties and townships; of the former there are four or five, but they are exceedingly small; of the latter between twenty and thirty; the towns themselves

* See Appendix, No 1.

are inconsiderable villages: however, they send members to the assembly, in the whole about seventy. The number of inhabitants, with negroes, and Indians, of which in this province there are several hundreds, amounts to 35,000. As the province affords but few commodities for exportation, horses, provisions, and an inconsiderable quantity of grain, with spermaceti candles, being the chief articles, they are obliged to Connecticut, and the neighbouring colonies, for most of their traffic; and by their means they carry on an extensive trade. Their mode of commerce is this: they trade to Great Britain, Holland, Africa, the West Indies, and the neighbouring colonies; from each of which places they import the following articles: from Great Britain, dry goods; from Holland, money; from Africa, slaves; from the West Indies, sugars, coffee, and molasses; and from the neighbouring colonies, lumber and provisions: and with what they purchase in one place they make their returns in another. Thus with the money they get in Holland, they pay their merchants in London; the sugars they procure in the West Indies, they carry to Holland; the slaves they fetch from Africa they send to the West Indies, together with lumber and provisions, which they get from the neighbouring colonies; the rum that they distill they export to Africa; and with the dry goods, which they purchase in London, they traffic in the neighbouring colonies. By this kind of circular commerce they subsist and grow rich. They have besides these some other inconsiderable branches of trade, but nothing worth mentioning. They have very few manufactures; they distill rum and make spermaceti candles; but in the article of dry goods, they are far behind the people of New York and Pennsylvania.

The government of this province is entirely democratical, every officer, except the collector of the customs, being appointed, I believe, either immediately by the people, or by the general assembly. The people choose annually a governor, lieutenant-governor, and ten assistants, which constitute an upper house. The representatives, or lower house, are elected every half year. These jointly have the appointment of all other public officers, (except the recorder, treasurer, and attorney-general, which are appointed likewise annually by the people) both military and civil; are invested with the powers of legislation, of regulating the militia, and of performing all other acts of government. The governor has no negative, but votes with the assistants, and in case of an equality has a casting voice. The assembly, or two houses united, are obliged to sit immediately after each election; at Newport in the summer, and in the winter alternately at Providence and South Kingston in Narraganset: they adjourn themselves, but may be called together, notwithstanding such adjournment, upon any urgent occasion by the governor. No assistant, or representative, is allowed any salary or pay for his attendance or service.

There are several courts of judicature. The assembly nominates annually so many justices for each township, as are deemed necessary. These have power to join people in matrimony, and to exercise other acts of authority usually granted to this order of magistrates. Any two of them may hear causes concerning small debts and trespasses; and three may try criminals for thefts, not exceeding ten pounds currency. Appeals in civil causes are allowed to the inferior courts of common-pleas; in criminal ones to the sessions of the peace; and in these the determinations are final. The sessions are held in each county twice every year by five or more justices; they adjudge all matters relating to the preservation of the peace, and the punishment of criminals, except in cases of death. Appeals are allowed from this court, in all causes that have originated in it, to the superior one. The inferior courts of common-pleas sit twice every year in each county, and are held by three or more justices. They take cognizance of all civil causes whatsoever, triable at common law; and if any one thinks himself aggrieved here, he may appeal to the superior one; which is held also annually twice in each county, by three judges, and which exercises all the authority of a court of king's-bench, common-pleas, and exchequer. The dernier resort is to the king in council, but this only in cases of

300 l. value, new tenor. The people have the power of pardoning criminals, except in cases of piracy, murder, or high treason; and then it is doubted whether they can even reprieve.

There is no established form of religion here; but Church of England men, independents, Quakers, Anabaptists, Moravians, Jews, and all other sects whatsoever, have liberty to exercise their several professions. The Society for the Propagation of the Gospel sends only four missionaries.

Arts and sciences are almost unknown, except to some few individuals; and there are no public seminaries of learning; nor do the Rhode Islanders in general seem to regret the want of them. The institution of a library society, which has lately taken place, may possibly in time produce a change in these matters.

The character of the Rhode Islanders is by no means engaging, or amiable, a circumstance principally owing to their form of government. Their men in power, from the highest to the lowest, are dependent upon the people, and frequently act without that strict regard to probity and honour, which ought invariably to influence and direct mankind. The private people are cunning, deceitful, and selfish: they live almost entirely by unfair and illicit trading. Their magistrates are partial and corrupt: and it is folly to expect justice in their courts of judicature; for he who has the greatest influence is generally found to have the fairest cause.* Were the governor to interpose his authority, were he to refuse to grant flags of truce,† or not to wink at abuses, he would at the expiration of the year be excluded from his office, the only thing perhaps which he has to subsist upon. Were the judges to act with impartiality, and to decide a cause to the prejudice or disadvantage of any great or popular leader, they would probably never be re-elected; indeed, they are incapable in general of determining the merits of a suit, for they are exceedingly illiterate, and, where they have nothing to make them partial, are managed almost entirely by the lawyers. In short, to give an idea of the wretched state of this colony, it has happened more than once that a person has had sufficient influence to procure a fresh emission of paper-money, solely to defraud his creditors: for having perhaps borrowed a considerable sum of

* The form of their judical oath, or affirmation (says Douglas, in his Summary), does not invoke the judgments of the omniscient God, who sees in secret, but only upon peril of the penalty of perjury. This does not seem (adds the same author in a note) to be a sacred or solemn oath, and may be illustrated by the story of two profligate thieves; one of them had stolen something, and told his friend of it: well, says his friend, but did any body see you ? No then, says his friend, it is yours as much as if you had bought it with your money. Vol. ii p. 95.

† It was usual during the late war for several governors in North America, on receiving a pecuniary consideration, to grant to the merchants flags of truce, by which they were licensed to go to the French West Indian Islands, in order to exchange prisoners The real scope and design of the voyage was, to carry on a prohibited

money, when the difference of exchange has been
1,200 per cent. he has afterward, under sanction of
the law, repaid only the same nominal sum in new
currency, when the difference has amounted perhaps to 2,500 per cent. Such, alas! is the situation
and character of this colony. It is needless, after
this, to observe that it is in a very declining state,
for it is impossible that it should prosper under such
abuses. Its West Indian trade has diminished,
owing indeed, in some measure, to the other colonies
having entered more largely into this lucrative branch
of commerce. it has lost during the war, by the enemy,
above 150 vessels: its own privateers, and it has generally had a great many, have had very ill success:
having kept up a regiment of provincial troops, it has
also been loaded with taxes, and many of the people
have been oppressed by the mode of collecting them:
for, the assembly having determined the quota of
each township, the inhabitants have been assessed

trade with the French, and to supply them with stores and provisions. Two or three prisoners were sufficient to cover the design; and in order to have a store in readiness, they seldom carried
more. By this abuse both governors and merchants acquired
great riches. Very plausible arguments indeed might be adduced
against prohibiting, or even restraining a commerce of that nature·
but as the wisdom of government did think fit, and probably with
better reason, to forbid it, nothing could excuse the corrupt and
mercenary spirit of those governors, who presumed to connive at
and encourage it. The Honourable Francis Fauquier, lieutenant-
governor of Virginia, who, amongst some few others, never could
be prevailed upon to countenance it, refused at one time an offer
of near 200 l. for the grant of a permit to make a single voyage.

by the town council*, consisting of the assistants residing there, the justices of the town, and a few freeholders elected annually by the freemen; and these
have been generally partial in their assessments, as
must necessarily happen under a combination of
such circumstances. After having said so much to
the disadvantage of this colony, I should be guilty
of injustice and ingratitude, were I not to declare
that there are many worthy gentlemen in it, who see
the misfortunes of their country, and lament them;
who are sensible that they arise from the wretched
nature of the government, and wish to have it altered;
who are courteous and polite, kind and hospitable
to strangers, and capable of great acts of generosity
and goodness, as I myself experienced during a very
severe fit of sickness which I lay under at this place.
The paper-money here is as bad as it is possible
to be, the difference of exchange being at least 2,500
per cent.

The 4th of September I took leave of Newport,
and having crossed over the river at Bristol Ferry,
where it is about a mile broad, and two other incon-

---

* Each township is managed by a town council, consisting of
the assistants who reside in the town, the justices of the town, and
six freeholders chosen annually by the freemen of the town, the
major part of them is a quorum, with full power to manage the
affairs and interest of the town to which they respectively belong,
to grant licenses to public houses, and are a probate office for
proving wills, and granting administration, with appeal to governor and council, as supreme ordinary. Douglas's Summary,
vol. ii. p. 85.

siderable ferries, I arrived in the evening at Providence. This is the chief town of what was formerly called Providence Plantation in Narraganset, and is at present the second considerable town in the province of Rhode Island. It is situated upon a pretty large river, and is distant from Newport about thirty miles. In the morning I set out for Boston, and arrived there about sunset, after a journey of five and forty miles. The country which I travelled over is chiefly grazing ground, laid out into neat enclosures, surrounded with stone walls, and rows of pseudo acacia or locust-trees, which are said with their leaves to manure and fertilize the land. I passed over a beautiful fall of water in Pawtucket river, upon a bridge, which is built directly over it. The fall is about twenty feet high, through several chasms in a rock, which runs diametrically across it, and serves as a dam to hold up the water. There are two or three mills, which have been erected for the advantage of having the different spouts or streams of water conducted to their respective wheels. These have taken very much from the beauty of the scene, which would otherwise be transcendantly elegant; for the fall, though not large or upon a great scale, is by far the most romantic and picturesque of any that I met with in my tour.

During the course of my ride from Newport, I observed prodigious flights of wild pigeons*: they

* See Appendix, No. 1.

directed their course to the southward, and the hemisphere was never entirely free from them. They are birds of passage, of beautiful plumage, and are excellent eating. The accounts given of their numbers are almost incredible; yet they are so well attested, and the opportunities of proving the truth of them are so frequent, as not to admit of their being called in question. Towards evening they generally settle upon trees, and sit one upon another in such crowds, as sometimes to break down the largest branches. The inhabitants at such times go out with long poles, and knock numbers of them on the head upon the roost; for they are either so fatigued by their flight, or terrified by the obscurity of the night, that they will not move, or take wing, without some great and uncommon noise to alarm them. I met with scarcely any other food at the ordinaries where I put up: and during their flight, the common people subsist almost wholly upon them.

Boston, the metropolis of Massachusetts Bay, in New England, is one of the largest and most flourishing towns in North America. It is situated upon a peninsula, or rather an island joined to the continent by an isthmus or narrow neck of land half a mile in length, at the bottom of a spacious and noble harbour, defended from the sea by a number of small islands. The length of it is nearly two miles, and the breadth of it half a one; and it is supposed to contain 3,000 houses, and 18 or 20,000 inhabitants.

Boston

At the entrance of the harbour stands a very good light-house; and upon an island, about a league from the town, a considerable castle, mounting near 150 cannon: there are several good batteries about it, and one in particular very strong, built by Mr. Shirley.* There are also two batteries in the town, for 16 or 20 guns each; but they are not, I believe, of any force. The buildings in Boston are in general good; the streets are open and spacious, and well paved; and the whole has much the air of some of our best country towns in England The country round about it is exceedingly delightful, and from a hill, which stands close to the town, where there is a beacon to alarm the neighbourhood in case of any surprise, is one of the finest prospects, the most beautifully variegated, and richly grouped, of any without exception that I have ever seen.

The chief public buildings are, three churches; thirteen or fourteen meeting-houses; the governor's palace; the court-house, or exchange; Faneuil Hall; a linen manufacturing-house; a work-house; a bride-well; a public granary; and a very fine wharf, at least half a mile long, undertaken at the expense of a number of private gentlemen, for the advantage of unloading and loading vessels. Most of these build-ings are handsome: the church, called King's Chapel, is exceedingly elegant; and fitted up in the Corin-thian taste There is also an elegant private con-

* See Note XIX.

cert-room highly finished in the Ionic manner. I had reason to think the situation of Boston unhealthy, at least in this season of the year, as there were frequent funerals every night during my stay there.

The situation of the province of Massachusetts Bay, including the district of Plymouth,* is between the 41st and 43d degree of north latitude, and about 72 degrees west longitude. The climate, soil, natural produce, and improved state of it, are much the same as of Rhode Island. It is divided into counties, and townships;† and each township, if it contains forty freeholders, ‡ has a right to send a member to the assembly;¶ the present number of

---

* Sagadahoc and the Maine, very large territories, lying north of New Hampshire, belong also to the province of Massachusetts Bay, they were annexed to it by the new charter of 1691. The Maine forms one county called the county of York, and sends three members to the council; Sagadahoc, which is annexed to it, sends one

† Townships are generally six miles square, and divided into sixty-three equal lots, viz. one lot for the first settled minister as inheritance, one lot for the ministry or glebe-lands, one lot for the benefit of a school, the other sixty lots to sixty persons or families, who, within five years from the grant, are to erect a dwelling-house, and clear seven acres of land, fit for mowing or ploughing, etc.

‡ By the charter, every freeholder should possess 40 s. freehold, or 50 l. personal estate; but I believe this article has not been strictly adhered to.

¶ Every town, containing forty freeholders, has a "right" to send a member to the assembly, but is not absolutely "obliged" to do so, unless it contains eighty freeholders.

representatives amounts to between 130 and 140, of which Boston sends four.

The number of souls in this province is supposed to amount to 200,000; and 40,000 of them to be capable of bearing arms. They carry on a considerable traffic, chiefly in the manner of the Rhode Islanders; but have some material articles for exportation, which the Rhode Islanders have not, except in a very trifling degree: these are salt fish, and vessels. Of the latter they build annually a great number, and send them, laden with cargoes of the former, to Great Britain, where they sell them. They clear out from Boston, Salem, Marblehead, and the different ports in this province, yearly, about * ton of shipping. Exclusive of these articles, their manufactures are not large; those of spirits, fish-oil, and iron, are, I believe, the most considerable. They fabricate beaver-hats, which they sell for a moidore apiece; and some years ago they erected a manufactory, with a design to encourage the Irish settlers to make linens; but at the breaking out of the war the price of labour was enhanced so much, that it was impossible to carry it on. Like the rest of the colonies they also endeavour to make woollens; but they have not yet been able to bring them to any degree of perfection; indeed it is an article in which I think they will not easily succeed; for the American wool is not only coarse, but in comparison of the

* See Appendix, No. 2.

English, exceedingly short. Upon the best inquiry I could make, I was not able to discover that any one had ever seen a staple of American wool longer than seven inches; whereas in the counties of Lincoln and Leicester, they are frequently twenty-two* inches long. In the southern colonies, at least in those parts where I travelled, there is scarcely any herbage;† and whether it is owing to this, or to the excessive heats, I am ignorant, the wool is short and hairy. The northern colonies have indeed greater plenty of herbage, but are for some months covered with snow; and without a degree of attention and care in housing the sheep, and guarding them against accidents, and wild beasts, which would not easily be compensated, it would be very difficult to increase their numbers to any great amount. The Americans seem conscious of this fact, and, notwithstanding a very severe prohibition, contrive to procure from England every year a considerable number of rams, in order to improve and multiply the breed. What the lands beyond the Allegheny and upon the banks of the Ohio may be, I do not know; they are said to be very rich: but the climate I believe is not less severe; and I think, upon collating different accounts, that the severity of heat and cold is not much abated by cultivation. The

* The common average length, I am told, is about sixteen inches.

† I speak of the country in general, in particular spots, as at Greenway Court, the herbage is very fine and luxuriant.

air becomes dryer and more wholesome, in proportion as the woods are cut down, and the ground is cleared and cultivated; but the cold is not less piercing, nor the snow less frequent.   I think therefore upon the whole, that America, though it may with particular care and attention, produce small quantities of tolerably good wool, will yet never be able to produce it in such plenty and of such a quality as to serve for the necessary consumption of its inhabitants.

The government of this province is lodged in the hands of a governor or lieutenant-governor, appointed by the king; a council of twenty-eight persons, chosen annually, with the governor's approbation, by the general assembly;* and a house of representatives † annually elected by the freeholders. The governor commissions all the militia, and other military officers; and, with consent of the council, also nominates and appoints all civil officers, except those that are concerned in the revenue.   He calls and adjourns the assembly, and has in every respect a very extensive authority.   His salary, with per-

* They are chosen by the new representatives, and the last year's counsellor; so that each counsellor has a vote in his own re-election. The governor has a negative to every counsellor's election, without being obliged to assign a reason.

† Each representative must be resident in the township for which he is elected, he must also have a plurality of votes respecting the number of voters, and not in comparison only of the other candidates, he is paid for his attendance and services, and subject to a fine if he neglects them.

quisites, amounts to about 1,300 l. sterling per year. The governor and council together have the probate of wills, and the power of granting administrations and divorces.

There are several courts of judicature. All actions under twenty shillings sterling are cognizable by a justice of peace, from whose determination there lies an appeal to the inferior county court of common-pleas; and from hence to the superior provincial court in its circuits, which is also a court of oyer and terminer in criminal affairs, and is held by a chief justice and some assistant judges. In this court, if the determination is not satisfactory, a rehearing of the cause may be had with a different jury;* and even, by petition to the general assembly, a second rehearing: the dernier resort is to his majesty in council, but this only in cases of 300 l. sterling value: and the appeal must be made within fourteen days after judgment.

The established religion here, as in all the other provinces of New England, is that of the Congregationalists; a religion, different in some trifling articles, though none very material, from the Presbyterian. There are, besides these however, great numbers of people of different persuasions, particularly of the religion of the Church of England, which seems to gain ground, and to become more fashion-

* Juries are, I believe, appointed partly by lot, and partly by rotation.

able every day. A church has been lately erected
at Cambridge, within sight of the college; which has
greatly alarmed the Congregationalists, who consider it as the most fatal stroke that could possibly
have been levelled at their religion. The building
is elegant, and the minister of it (the Reverend Mr.
Apthorpe,) is a young man of shining parts, great
learning, and pure and engaging manners.*

Arts and Sciences seem to have made a greater
progress here, than in any other part of America.
Harvard College has been founded above a hundred
years; and although it is not upon a perfect plan,
yet it has produced a very good effect. The arts are
undeniably forwarder in Massachusetts Bay than
either in Pennsylvania or New York. The public
buildings are more elegant; and there is a more general turn for music, painting, and the belles lettres.

The character of the inhabitants of this province
is much improved, in comparison of what it was:
but Puritanism and a spirit of persecution is not yet
totally extinguished. The gentry of both sexes are
hospitable, and good-natured; there is an air of
civility in their behaviour, but it is constrained by
formality and preciseness. Even the women, though
easiness of carriage is peculiarly characteristic of

* This gentleman, I have heard, afterward met with so much
opposition and persecution from the Congregationalists, that he
was obliged to resign his cure, to quit the colony, and has since
lived in England upon a living, (I believe in Surrey) which was
given him by the late Archbishop Secker.

their nature, appear here with more stiffness and reserve than in the other colonies. They are formed with symmetry, are handsome, and have fair and delicate complections; but are said universally, and even proverbially, to have very indifferent teeth.

The lower class of the people are more in the extreme of this character; and, which is constantly mentioned as singularly peculiar to them, are impertinently curious and inquisitive. I was told of a gentleman of Philadelphia, who, in travelling through the provinces of New England, having met with many impertinences from this extraordinary turn of character, at length fell upon an expedient almost as extraordinary, to get rid of them. He had observed, when he went into an ordinary,* that every individual of the family had a question or two to propose to him relative to his history, and that, till each was satisfied, and they had conferred and compared together their information, there was no possibility of procuring any refreshment. He, therefore, the moment he went into any of these places, inquired for the master, the mistress, the sons, the daughters, the men-servants and the maid-servants; and having assembled them all together, he began in this manner: "Worthy people, I am B. F.† of "Philadelphia, by trade a ——, and a bachelor; "I have some relations at Boston, to whom I am

* Inns are so called in America.

† Benjamin Franklin.

"going to make a visit: my stay will be short, and
"I shall then return and follow my business, as a
"prudent man ought to do. This is all I know of
"myself, and all I can possibly inform you of; I beg
"therefore that you will have pity upon me and my
"horse, and give us both some refreshment."

Singular situations and manners will be productive of singular customs; but frequently such as upon slight examination may appear to be the effects of mere grossness of character, will, upon deeper research, be found to proceed from simplicity and innocence. A very extraordinary method of courtship, which is sometimes practised amongst the lower people of this province, and is called Tarrying, has given occasion to this reflection.* When a man is enamoured of a young woman, and wishes to marry her, he proposes the affair to her parents, (without whose consent no marriage in this colony can take place); if they have no objection, they allow him to tarry with her one night, in order to make his court to her. At their usual time the old couple retire to bed, leaving the young ones to settle matters as they can, who, after having sat up as long as they think proper, get into bed together also, but without pulling off their under-garments, in order to prevent scandal. If the parties agree, it is all very well; the banns are published, and they are married without delay. If not, they part, and possibly never see

* See Note XX.

each other again; unless, which is an accident that seldom happens, the forsaken fair-one prove pregnant, and then the man is obliged to marry her, under pain of excommunication.*

The province of Massachusetts Bay has been for some years past, I believe, rather on the decline. Its inhabitants have lost several branches of trade, which they are not likely to recover again. They formerly supplied, not only Connecticut, but other parts of the continent, with dry goods, and received specie in return: but since the introduction of paper currency they have been deprived of great part of this commerce. Their ship trade is considerably decreased, owing to their not having been so careful in the construction of vessels as formerly· their

* A gentleman some time ago travelling upon the frontiers of Virginia, where there are few settlements, was obliged to take up his quarters one evening at a miserable plantation, where, exclusive of a negro or two, the family consisted of a man and his wife, and one daughter about sixteen years of age. Being fatigued, he presently desired them to shew him where he was to sleep; accordingly they pointed to a bed in a corner of the room where they were sitting. The gentleman was a little embarrassed but, being excessively weary, he retired, half undressed himself, and got into bed. After some time the old gentlewoman came to bed to him, after her the old gentleman, and last of all the young lady. This, in a country excluded from all civilized society, could only proceed from simplicity and innocence· and indeed it is a general and true observation that forms and observances become necessary and are attended to, in proportion as manners become corrupt, and it is found expedient to guard against vice, and that design and duplicity of character, which, from the nature of things, will ever prevail in large and cultivated societies

fisheries too have not been equally successful: they have had also a considerable number of provincial troops* in pay during the course of the present war, and have been burthened with heavy taxes. These have been laid upon estates, real and personal. Some merchants in Boston, I have been credibly informed, have paid near 400 l. sterling annually. Assessments are made by particular officers, who, with the selectmen, constables, overseers, and several others, are elected annually by the freemen, for the direction and management of each particular township.

There is less paper money in this colony, than in any other of America: the current coin is chiefly gold and silver: and Boston is the only place, I believe, where there ever was a mint to coin money.

I was told of a very impolitic law in force in this province, which forbids any master, or commander of a vessel, to bring strangers into the colony, without giving security that they shall not become chargeable to it.

However, notwithstanding what has been said, Massachusetts Bay is a rich, populous, and well-cultivated province.

I cannot take leave of it without relating a very extraordinary story, communicated to me by persons of undoubted credit, as it further tends to illustrate the character and manners of its inhabitants.

* Between six and seven thousand, I believe

Some years ago a commander of one of his majesty's ships of war being stationed at this place, had orders to cruise from time to time, in order to protect our trade, and distress the enemy. It happened unluckily that he returned from one of his cruises on a Sunday; and as he had left his lady at Boston, the moment she heard of the ship's arrival, she hasted down to the water's side, in order to receive him. The captain, on landing, embraced her with tenderness and affection: this, as there were several spectators by, gave great offence, and was considered as an act of indecency, and a flagrant profanation of the Sabbath. The next day, therefore, he was summoned before the magistrates, who with many severe rebukes and pious exhortations, ordered him to be publicly whipped. The captain stifled his indignation and resentment as much as possible; and as the punishment, from the frequency of it, was not attended with any great degree of ignominy or disgrace, he mixed with the best company, was well received by them, and they were apparently good friends. At length the time of the station expired, and he was recalled: he went, therefore, with seeming concern, to take leave of his worthy friends; and that they might spend one more happy day together before their final separation, he invited the principal magistrates and selectmen to dine with him on board his ship, upon the day of his departure. They accepted the invitation, and nothing could be more joyous and convivial than the entertainment which he gave them. At length the fatal moment arrived that was to separate them: the anchor was apeak, the sails were unfurled, and nothing was wanting but the signal to get under way.* The captain, after taking an affectionate leave of his worthy friends, accompanied them upon deck, where the boatswain and crew were in readiness to receive them. He there thanked them afresh for the civilities they had shown him, of which, he said, he should retain an eternal remembrance, and to which he wished it had been in his power to have made a more adequate return. One point of civility only remained to be adjusted between them, which, as it was in his power, so he meant most fully to recompense to them. He then reminded them of what had passed, and ordering the crew to pinion them, had them brought one by one to the gang-way, where the boatswain stripped off their shirts, and with a cat of nine tails laid on the back of each forty stripes save one. They were then, amidst the shouts and acclamations of the crew, shoved into their boats: and the captain immediately getting under way, sailed for England.†

* This is usually written, "under weigh"· but I am extremely doubtful of the propriety of the phrase.

† This story has lately appeared in one of the English newspapers, told with much humour, and with some difference respecting the occasion and mode of the captain's punishment. The

The 12th of October I embarked on board his majesty's ship the Winchester, of fifty guns, Captain Hale commander, for the river Piscataqua, in New Hampshire; and we came to an anchor there the next day, after a pleasant passage.

The capital of this province is Portsmouth, which is situated upon the river: it is an inconsiderable place, and chiefly built of wood. Very little can be said of the province of New Hampshire, materially different from what has been said of Massachusets Bay. The climate, produce, trade, government, religion, and manners of it are much the same. There are supposed to be about 40,000 inhabitants, 8,000 militia, and 6 or 700 provincial troops. There are only two missionaries of the Church of England, and one of these has lately applied to be removed to Rhode Island. The chief articles for exportation are fish, cattle, ships, of which they annually build near 200*, and masts for the royal navy. These are made of the white pine, and are, I believe, the finest in the world, many of them being forty yards long, and as many inches in diameter. They never cut them down but in times of deep snow, as it would be impossible in any other season to get them down to the river When the trees are fallen, they yoke

author cannot take upon himself to say which account may be most exact, but he has chosen to abide by that which he heard at Boston. They either of them serve to characterize the people, and to answer the author's purpose in relating it.

* See Appendix, No. 2.

seventy or eighty pair of oxen, and drag them along the snow. It is exceedingly difficult to put them first into motion, which they call raising them; and when they have once effected this, they never stop upon any account whatsoever till they arrive at the water's side. Frequently some of the oxen are taken ill, upon which they immediately cut them out of the gears; and are sometimes obliged, I was told, to destroy five or six pair of them. The forests, where these masts grow, are reserved to the crown, which appoints a surveyor of them, who is commonly the governor of this province. This is not the only expedient employed by government for the preservation of such trees as may be of use for the royal navy; for there is an act of parliament, I believe, which prohibits, under pain of certain fines and penalties, the cutting down, or destroying of any white pine-tree, of specified dimensions, not growing within the boundaries of any township, without his majesty's license, in any of the provinces of New England, New York, or New Jersey. a restriction absolutely necessary, whether considered as securing a provision for the navy, or as a check upon that very destructive practice, taken from the Indians, of fire-hunting. It used to be the custom for large companies to go into the woods in the winter, and to set fire to the brush and underwood, in a circle of several miles. This circle gradually contracting itself, the deer, and other wild animals, enclosed, naturally retired from the flames, till at length they got herded together in a very small compass. Then, blinded and suffocated by the smoke, and scorched by the fire, which every moment came nearer to them, they forced their way, under the greatest trepidation and dismay, through flames; and were no sooner got into the open daylight again, than they were shot by the hunters, who stood without, and were in readiness to fire upon them. The trees included within the circle, although not absolutely burnt down, were so dried and injured, that they never vegetated any more: and as the fire did not only contract itself inwardly, but dilated also outwardly, and sometimes continued burning for several weeks, till rain, or some accidental circumstance put it out; it is incredible what injury and devastation it occasioned in the woods. I was once a spectator of a similar fire in Virginia, which had happened through accident. Nothing could be more awful and tremendous than the sight. It was of great extent, and burned several weeks before the inhabitants could subdue it. They effected it at last by cutting away the underwood, in wide and long avenues, to leeward of the fire, by which it was deprived of the means of communicating or spreading any farther. In Virginia (and, I believe, the other colonies), there is an express act of assembly, passed in the 12th year of his late majesty, to forbid this practice.

The province of New Hampshire, I was informed

at Portsmouth, has grown rich during the war, by the loss of its own vessels, they having been commonly insured above value.

The currency here is extremely bad, not better than that in Rhode Island.

Having travelled over so large a tract of this vast continent, before I bid a final farewell to it, I must beg the reader's indulgence, while I stop for a moment, and as it were from the top of a high eminence, take one general retrospective look at the whole. An idea, strange as it is visionary, has entered into the minds of the generality of mankind, that empire is travelling westward; and every one is looking forward with eager and impatient expectation to that destined moment when America is to give law to the rest of the world. But if ever an idea was illusory and fallacious, I am fully persuaded, that this will be so.

America is formed for happiness, but not for empire. in a course of 1,200 miles I did not see a single object that solicited charity; but I saw insuperable causes of weakness, which will necessarily prevent its being a potent state.

Our colonies may be distinguished into the southern and northern, separated from each other by the Susquehanna and that imaginary line which divides Maryland from Pennsylvania.

The southern colonies have so many inherent

causes of weakness, that they never can possess any real strength. The climate operates very powerfully upon them, and renders them indolent, inactive, and unenterprising; this is visible in every line of their character. I myself have been a spectator, and it is not an uncommon sight, of a man in the vigour of life, lying upon a couch, and a female slave standing over him, wafting off the flies, and fanning him, while he took his repose.

The southern colonies (Maryland, which is the smallest and most inconsiderable, alone excepted) will never be thickly seated: for as they are not confined within determinate limits, but extend to the westward indefinitely, men, sooner than apply to laborious occupations, occupations militating with their dispositions, and generally considered too as the inheritance and badge of slavery, will gradually retire westward, and settle upon fresh lands, which are said also to be more fertile; where, by the servitude of a negro or two, they may enjoy all the satisfaction of an easy and indolent independency: hence the lands upon the coast will of course remain thin of inhabitants.

The mode of cultivation by slavery, is another insurmountable cause of weakness. The number of negroes in the southern colonies is upon the whole nearly equal, if not superior, to that of the white men; and they propagate and increase even faster. Their condition is truly pitiable; their labour excessively hard, their diet poor and scanty, their treatment cruel and oppresive: they cannot therefore but be a subject of terror to those who so inhumanly tyrannize over them.

The Indians near the frontiers are a still further formidable cause of subjection. The southern Indians are numerous, and are governed by a sounder policy than formerly: experience has taught them wisdom. They never make war with the colonists without carrying terror and devastation along with them. They sometimes break up entire counties together. Such is the state of the southern colonies.

The northern colonies are of stronger stamina, but they have other difficulties and disadvantages to struggle with, not less arduous, or more easy to be surmounted, than what have been already mentioned. Their limits being defined, they will undoubtedly become exceedingly populous: for though men will readily retire back towards the frontiers of their own colony, yet they will not so easily be induced to settle beyond them, where different laws and polities prevail, and where, in short, they are a different people: but in proportion to want of territory, if we consider the proposition in a general and abstract light, will be want of power. But the northern colonies have still more positive and real disadvantages to contend with. They are composed of people of different nations, different manners, different religions, and different languages They have a mutual jealousy of each other, fomented by considerations of interest, power, and ascendancy. Religious zeal, too, like a smothered fire, is secretly burning in the hearts of the different sectaries that inhabit them, and were it not restrained by laws and superior authority, would soon burst out into a flame of universal persecution. Even the peaceable Quakers struggle hard for pre-eminence, and evince in a very striking manner that the passions of mankind are much stronger than any principles of religion.

The colonies, therefore, separately considered, are internally weak; but it may be supposed, that, by an union or coalition, they would become strong and formidable: but an union seems almost impossible: one founded in dominion or power is morally so: for, were not England to interfere, the colonies themselves so well understand the policy of preserving a balance, that, I think, they would not be idle spectators, were any one of them to endeavour to subjugate its next neighbour. Indeed, it appears to me a very doubtful point, even supposing all the colonies of America to be united under one head, whether it would be possible to keep in due order and government so wide and extended an empire, the difficulties of communication, of intercourse, of correspondence, and all other circumstances considered.

A voluntary association or coalition, at least a permanent one, is almost as difficult to be supposed: for fire and water are not more heterogeneous than the different colonies in North America. Nothing can exceed the jealousy and emulation which they possess in regard to each other. The inhabitants of Pennsylvania and New York have an inexhaustible source of animosity, in their jealousy for the trade of the Jerseys. Massachusetts Bay and Rhode Island, are not less interested in that of Connecticut. The West Indies are a common subject of emulation to them all. Even the limits and boundaries of each colony are a constant source of litigation. In short, such is the difference of character, of manners, of religion, of interest, of the different colonies, that I think, if I am not wholly ignorant of the human mind, were they left to themselves, there would soon be a civil war from one end of the continent to the other; while the Indians and negroes would, with better reason, impatiently watch the opportunity of exterminating them all together.

After all, however, supposing what I firmly believe will never take place, a permanent union or alliance of all the colonies, yet it could not be effectual, or productive of the event supposed; for such is the extent of coast settled by the American colonies that it can never be defended but by a maritime power: America must first be mistress of the sea before she can be independent, or mistress of herself. Suppose the colonies ever so populous; suppose them capable of maintaining 100,000 men constantly in arms, (a supposition in the highest degree extravagant), yet half a dozen frigates would with ease ravage and lay waste the whole country from end to end, without a possibility of their being able to prevent it; the country is so intersected by rivers, rivers of such magnitude as to render it impossible to build bridges over them, that all communication is in a manner cut off. An army under such circumstances could never act to any purpose or effect; its operations would be totally frustrated.

Further, a great part of the opulence and power of America depends upon her fisheries, and her commerce with the West Indies, she cannot subsist without them; but these would be entirely at the mercy of that power which might have the sovereignty of the seas. I conclude, therefore, that England, so long as she maintains her superiority in that respect, will also possess a superiority in America; but the moment she loses the empire of the one, she will be deprived of the sovereignty of the other: for were that empire to be held by France, Holland, or any other power, America, will, in all probability, be annexed to it. New establishments formed in the interior parts of America, will not come under this predicament; I should therefore think it the best policy to enlarge the present colonies, but not to establish fresh ones; for to suppose interior colonies to be of use to the mother country, by being a check upon those already settled, is to suppose what is contrary to experience, and the nature of things, viz.

that men removed beyond the reach of power will be subordinate to it.

October 20, I embarked again on board the Winchester, for England; and arrived in Plymouth Sound the 21st of November, after a rough and tempestuous voyage.

.

.

APPENDIX, N° 1.

CATALOGUE of several TREES, PLANTS, BIRDS, FISHES, ANIMALS, &c. mentioned in the course of this Work; with their Common Names, and the names given them by CATESBY and LINNÆUS.

COMMON NAMES.	CATESBEAN.	LINNÆAN.
Tobacco, ...		... Nicotiana.
Maize or Indian Corn, ...	Frumentum Indicum,	.... Zea Mays.
Rattle-Snake Root, ...	Aristolochia Pistolochia,	Polygala Senega.
Pigeon Plumb or Berry, .	Cerasus latiore folio.	
Hiccory, ...	Nux juglans alba Virginiensis, &c.	Juglans alba.
Pignut, . . .	Nux juglans Carolinensis, &c.	
Cypress-Tree, . . .	Cupressus Americana,	.Cupressus disticha.
Sugar Maple, . .	.. . .	Acer Saccharinum.
Red-Flowering Maple, ..	Acer Virginianum, &c...	...Acer Rubrum.
Candle-Berry Myrtle, ...	Myrtus, Brabanticæ similis Carolinensis, &c. .	Myrica Cerifera.
Virginian Cedar, ... ,..		Juniperus Virginiana.
Sassafras Tree,.. .	Cornus Mas Odorata,	...Laurus Sassafras.

COMMON NAMES.	CATESBEAN.	LINNÆAN.
Dogwood, ...	Cornus Mas Virginiana, &c.	{ Cornus Flor- ida.
Pseudo-acacia or Locust-tree,.	} Acacia, . .	Robinia Pseudo-acacia.
Honey Locust,.	Acacia, ..	.. Gleditsia.
Red-Bud, or Judas Tree, ...	} Siliquastrum, .	Cercis Canadensis
Fringe-Tree, ...	Amelanchior Virginiana, &c.	{ Chionanthus Virginica.
Tulip-Tree, ...	Arbor Tulipifera, &c. ..	{ Liriodendron Tulipifera
Umbrella-Tree, .	{ Magnolia amplissimo flore albo, &c.	{ Magnolia tripetala.
Sweet Flowering Bay, or Swamp Laurel . . .	} Magnolia lauri folio, &c.	Magnolia Glauca.
Trumpet Flower .	. Bignonia fraxini foliis, &c..	{ Lonicera sem- per virens.
Yellow Jasmine,	{ Gelsominum sive jasminum luteum, &c. .	{ Bignonia sem- per virens.
Catalpa,	Bignonia Urucu foliis, &c. .	Bignonia Catalpa
Chamædaphne, or Dwarf Laurel..	} Chamædaphne foliis tini, &c.	{ Kalmia lati- folia.
Chamædaphne .	Semper virens angustis foliis,	{ Kalmia An- gustifolia.

N. B. These are by the Virginians commonly called Ivy.

May Apple, . . .	Anapodophyllon Canadense, &c.	
Chinkapin, .	Castanea pumila Virginiana, &c	Fagus pumila
Persimon, ...		{ Diospyros Virginiana.
Scarlet Flowering Chestnut, . . .	} Pavia.	
Virginia Maple, ..	Platanus Occidentalis, .	{ Platanus Oc- cidentalis.

Appendix, N° 1

COMMON NAMES.   CATESBEAN.   LINNÆAN

Button Wood,.. .   ...{ Cephalantus
                                               Occidentalis.

Wild Oat, ...Zizania Aquatica.

Ginseng,.... .... .Aureliana Canadensis, ...{ Panax quin-
                                                 quefolium.

Tuckahoe Root,..   ....{ Lycoperdon
                                                  Tuber.

Pacoon Flower.
Atamusco Lilly,... Lillio Narcissus Virginiensis.
Pine Trees.
    White Pine, ...' . ...Pinus Strobus.

    Spruce Pine, ...{ Pinus foliis
                                              singularibus.

B I R D S.

Bald Eagle, ... Aquila capite albo.
Fishing Hawk,   .. . Accipiter Piscatorius.
Wild Turkey, .   Gallo Pavo Sylvestris.
Sorus, ... Gallinula Americana.
Partridge,..... Perdrix Sylvestris Virginiana.
Blue-Wing,.   Querquidula Americana fusca.
Shell-Drake.
Summer-Duck, Anas Americanus cristatus elegans.

Pigeon of Passage,   Palumbus migratorius, .{ Columba mi-
                                                gratoria.

Mocking-Bird, ..{ Turdus minor, cinereo { Turdus Poly-
                       albus non maculatus, . {   glottus.

Red-Bird, or Virginia } Coccothraustes ruber,˜. Loxia Cardinalis.
    Nightingale, ... }

Blue-Bird, ...Rubicula Americana cærulea..Motacilla Sialis.

[159]

COMMON NAMES.   CATESBEAN.   LINNÆAN.

Yellow-Bird, ...Parus luteus, &c Qu ?
Baltimore-Bird,.......Icterus ex aureo nigroque varius.
Humming-Bird,.   Mellivora Avis Carolinensis, { Trochilus Colubris.
Turtle,   .   ..Turtur Carolinensis.

FISH.

Grampus.
Porpess,.... ... . { Delphinus Phocæna.
Albecor,. .... { Scomber Thynnus.
Boneta, ... Scomber Pelamys.
Flying-Fish, ...Hirundo,...   ..... } Exocætusvolitans.
Sheepshead.
Rock-Fish.
Drums, ...Coracino affinis.
Shad,. . . .   Turdus cinereus peltatus; Qu ?
Black-Fish.
Sea-Bass.
Sturgeon,.....   .... Acipenser Sturio.

ANIMALS.

Buffalo, ... Bison Americanus.
Moose or Elk   Alce maxima Americana nigra.
Grey Fox,   .   Vulpis cinereus Americanus.
Flying Squirrel, ...Sciurus volans.

[160]

Appendix, N° I

COMMON NAMES.	CATESBEAN.	LINNÆAN.
Ground Squirrel,	. . . .Sciurus striatus.	
Skunk or Polecat,.	. Putorius Americanus striatus,	. . . . . .Putorius.

SNAKES, REPTILES, INSECTS, &c.

Rattle-Snake, .	. Vipera caudisona Americana,	. . .Crotalus.
Black-Snake,.	. . . . Anguis niger.	
Wampum-Snake,	Anguis e cæruleo et albo varius.	
Bead-Snake,...	. { Anguis niger, maculis rubris } et luteis eleganter varius.	
Bull-Frog, ...	Rana maxima Americana aquatica,	. Ocellata.
Green-Tree Frog,	. .Rana viridis arborea, ...	. Arborea.
Fire-Fly, . . .	. . . .	. . . Lampyris.
Mosquito,.	. . . .	. . . . .Culex pipiens.

APPENDIX, N° 2.

I HAVE not been able to procure any satisfactory account of the tonnage cleared out of the different ports
of North America, in the years 1759 and 1760; owing to
the incorrect manner of taking the tonnage at that time,
and the irregularity with which the accounts were generally
transmitted to England: but having been favoured by G.
Chalmers, Esq. first Clerk to the Committe of Council for
the consideration of all matters relating to trade and foreign
plantations, with an exact statement of the number of
vessels and their tonnage, which entered inwards and cleared
outwards, in Massachusetts, Pennsylvania, Virginia, and
South Carolina, in the year 1770; at which time the colonies
were in their most flourishing condition:—a probable con-
jecture may be formed from it of the state of their commerce
ten years before, by allowing for its increase during that
period of peace and prosperity. The number of vessels
and their tonnage cleared out from New York is not specified in the statement; but by collating other accounts I have
endeavoured to ascertain it as nearly as possible. Mr.
Chalmers, with the greatest liberality and politeness,
favoured me at the same time with several tables and statements relating to the commercial situation of the United
States, both before and since the American war, which, as
they are full of information, and cannot fail of being highly
interesting to the reader, I have here annexed: and I am

[162]

happy to have this opportunity of publicly expressing my gratitude and obligation to that gentleman, for his indulgence in permitting me to avail myself of such valuable information.

1.—A STATEMENT of the Number of VESSELS, with their TONNAGE, which entered Inwards and cleared Outwards, in the following Countries, during the Year 1770.

	Ships entered. Inwards.		Ships entered. Outw'ds.	
	Vessels.	Tons.	Vessels.	Tons.
Massachusetts	1,247	65,271	1,334	70,284
Pennsylvania	804	50,901	820	49,654
Virginia	613	44,803	604	45,179
South Carolina	492	29,504	492	32,031
In the same year, according to the best information which I have been able to procure, there cleared out from New York	......	......	..612	say 36,720

2.—VESSELS employed between GREAT BRITAIN and the Countries belonging to the UNITED STATES.

	Ships.	Tons.
Number and tonnage of the vessels clearing outwards, and employed yearly in the trade between Great Britain and the countries now belonging to the United States of America, on an average of the years 1770, 1771, and 1772 before the war......	628	81,951
Number of ditto so employed, entering inwards, on a like average	699	91,540
Medium of the average number and tonnage of the vessels entering inwards, and clearing outwards........................	663	86,745

	BRITISH.		AMERICAN.		TOTAL.	
	Ships.	Tons.	Ships.	Tons.	Ships.	Tons.
Number and tonnage of British vessels, and of vessels belonging to the United States, clearing outwards, so employed, on an average of the years 1787, 1788, and 1789, since the war	272	55,785	157	25,725	429	81,510
Number and tonnage of ditto, entering inwards, on a like average...	251	49,405	169	27,403	420	76,808
Medium of the average-number and tonnage of British and American vessels so employed, entering inwards and clearing outwards	261	52,595	163	26,564	425	79,159

It appears from the foregoing averages, that the number of vessels employed in the direct commercial intercourse between Great Britain and the countries now belonging to the United States of America, has decreased since the war 238; and that the quantity of tonnage has decreased since the war 7,586 tons. The decrease of the tonnage appears to be much less than the decrease of the number of the ships, and the decrease of the tonnage inwards is much greater than that of the tonnage outwards. The reason that the quantity of the tonnage in general appears to be less decreased than the number of ships, is,

FIRST.—That larger ships are now employed in this as well as in every other branch of commerce, than formerly.

SECONDLY.—The imperfect manner of taking the tonnage before the war, which, in order that the master might be charged a less sum for pilotage and lighthouse duties, was generally estimated at about one-third less than it really was.

The greater decrease of the tonnage inwards, compared with that of the tonnage outwards, is to be imputed to the diminished importation of the bulky articles of rice and tobacco.

It appears by the foregoing account of the vessels employed in this trade since the war, that the number of American vessels so employed, 68 ships; and the quantity of British tonnage so employed, exceeds the quantity of American tonnage so employed, 26,031 tons.

As there was no distinction before the war, between ships belonging to the inhabitants of the countries now under the dominion of the United States and the other parts of the British dominions, it is impossible to state with certainty, what was the proportion of each description of ships then employed in this branch of commerce

The vessels so employed, were then of three sorts:

FIRST—Vessels belonging to merchants resident in the British European dominions.

SECONDLY—Vessels belonging to British merchants, occasionally resident in those colonies that now form the United States.

THIRDLY—Vessels belonging to merchants, who were natives and permanent inhabitants of those colonies that now form the United States.

Appendix, N° 2

3.—The following TABLE will shew the PROPORTION of each Description of Vessels, classed in the Manner before mentioned, then employed in this Branch of Commerce, according to the best Information that can be obtained:

	Proportion of vessels belonging to merchants, resident in the British European dominions.	Proportion of vessels belonging to British merchants, occasionally resident in those Colonies that now form the United States.	Proportion of vessels belonging to merchants, who were natives and permanent inhabitants of those Colonies that now form the United States.
New England, .	1 - 8th	1 - 8th.	6 - 8ths
New York, ...	3 - 8ths.	3 - 8ths.	2 - 8ths.
Pennsylvania, .	2 - 8ths	3 - 8ths.	3 - 8ths.
Maryland and Virginia,	6 - 8ths.	1 - 8th.	1 - 8th.
North Carolina, .	5 - 8ths.	2 - 8ths.	1 - 8th.
S. Carolina and Georgia,	5 - 8ths.	2 - 8ths.	1 - 8th.

From the foregoing table it is evident, that the proportion of vessels, classed under the before-mentioned descriptions, varied according to the different colonies, now forming the United States, with which the Commerce of Great Britain was then carried on; the quantity of shipping so employed, which belonged either to the inhabitants of Great Britain, or to British merchants occasionally resident in the said colonies, being much greater in the commercial intercourse then carried on with the southern colonies, than with the northern colonies, particularly those of New England. But upon the whole, there is reason to believe, from

[167]

calculations founded on the foregoing table, as well as from other information, that the proportion of tonnage, employed before the war in this branch of commerce, which belonged to the inhabitants of Great Britain, was about four-eighths and an half; and the proportion, which belonged to British merchants, occasionally resident in the colonies now forming the United States, was about one-eighth and an half, making together nearly six-eighths of the whole; and that the proportion of tonnage so employed, which belonged to merchants, who were then natives and permanent inhabitants of the colonies now forming the United States, was rather more than two-eighths of the whole. At present the proportion of tonnage, employed in this branch of conmerce, belonging to the merchants of Great Britain, is nearly six-eighths of the whole; and the proportion of tonnage, belonging to the merchants of the United States, is rather more than two-eighths of the whole; so that in this view of the subject, though the quantity of shipping, employed between Great Britain, and the countries now under the dominion of the United States, has since the war decreased on the whole; yet, allowing for this decrease, the share of the shipping which belongs to the merchants of Great Britain, has increased in the proportion of one-eighth and an half; (the share of the shipping, which before the war belonged to British merchants, occasionally resident in the colonies now forming the United States, being transferred to merchants resident in Great Britain); and the share of the shipping so employed, which now belongs to merchants, subjects of the United States, and permanent inhabitants thereof, is nearly the same as it was before the war.

Appendix, N° 2

4.—VESSELS employed between GREAT BRITAIN and the remaining BRITISH COLONIES in NORTH AMERICA.

	Ships.	Tons.
Number and tonnage of British vessels clearing outwards, and employed yearly in the trade between Great Britain and the remaining British colonies in North America, on an average of the years 1770, 1771, and 1772, before the war.	250	9,582
Number and tonnage of ditto so employed, entering inwards, on a like average. . . .	273	12,857
Medium of the average number and tonnage of British vessels entering inwards, and clearing outwards	261	11,219
Number and tonnage of British vessels clearing outwards, employed in this trade, on an average of the years 1787, 1788, and 1789, since the war.	486	61,858
Number and tonnage of ditto so employed, entering inwards, on a like average . .	249	30,355
Medium of the average number and tonnage of British vessels entering inwards, and clearing outwards. . . .	367	46,106

By the foregoing averages it appears, that the number of vessels employed between Great Britain and the remaining colonies in North America, being all British ships, has increased since the war in the proportion of about one-half, being 106 vessels more than it was before the war; and the quantity of tonnage has increased 34,887 tons, being in the proportion of about four times more than it was before the war.

5.—VESSELS employed between the remaining BRITISH COLONIES in NORTH AMERICA, and the countries belonging to the UNITED STATES.

	Ships	Tons
Number and tonnage of British vessels clearing outwards, and employed yearly in the trade between the remaining British colonies in North America, and the countries which were then British colonies, but now form the United States of America, on an average of the years 1770, 1771, and 1772, before the war	250	9,582
Number and tonnage of ditto so employed, entering inwards, on a like average	276	12,857
Medium of the average number and tonnage of British vessels entering inwards, and clearing outwards.	263	11,219
Number and tonnage of British vessels clearing outwards, and employed yearly in the trade between the remaining British colonies in North America, and the countries belonging to the United States, on an average of the years 1787, 1788, and 1789, since the war	208	15,135
Number and tonnage of ditto so employed, entering inwards, on a like average .	269	15,524
Medium of the average number and tonnage of British vessels entering inwards, and clearing outwards	238	15,329

The number of the vessels, so stated, includes their repeated voyages, and it appears that the number has decreased, since the war, 25 vessels, or about one-tenth. but the quantity of the tonnage has increased 4,110 tons, or about one-third. The vessels, employed before the war in this branch of trade, might lawfully belong to the inhabitants of the countries now under the dominion of the United States, it is certain they then owned much the greatest share of these vessels: but vessels so employed can now belong only to the inhabitants of the remaining colonies, or of some other part of the British dominions.

6.—VESSELS employed between the BRITISH ISLANDS in the WEST INDIES, and the Countries belonging to the UNITED STATES.

	Ships.	Tons.
Number and tonnage of British vessels clearing outwards, and employed yearly in the trade between the British Islands in the West Indies, and the countries belonging to theUnited States, on an average of the years 1770, 1771, and 1772, before the war......	2,172	103,540
Number and tonnage of ditto so employed, entering inwards, on a like average........	2,297	111,939
Medium of the average number and tonnage of British vessels entering inwards, and clearing outwards.....................	2,234	107,739
Number and tonnage of British vessels clearing outwards, and employed yearly in the trade between the British islands in the West Indies, and the countries belonging to the United States, on an average of the years 1787, 1788, and 1789, since the war......	510	57,904
Number and tonnage of ditto so employed, entering in wards, on a like average......	579	67,573
Medium of the average number and tonnage of British vessels, entering inwards, and clearing outwards.....................	544	62,738

THE account of the number of vessels from whence these averages are taken, includes their repeated voyages. It has decreased since the war 1,690 ships, or is three-fourths less than it was before the war. The quantity of tonnage has decreased 45,001 tons, or rather less than half what it was before the war: but five-eighths of these vessels, before the war, belonged to merchants, permanent inhabitants of the countries now under the dominion of the United States; and three-eighths to British merchants, residing occasionally in the said countries. At that time very few vessels belonging to British merchants, resident in the British European dominions, or in the British islands in the West Indies, had a share in this trade. The vessels employed in this trade can now only belong to British subjects residing in the present British dominions. Many vessels now go from the ports of Great Britain, carrying British manufactures to the United States, then load with lumber and provisions for the British islands in the West Indies, and return, with the produce of these islands, to Great Britain. The vessels so employed are much larger than those in which this trade was formerly carried on, and for this reason the tonnage employed in it has decreased much less than the number of the vessels.

7.—VESSELS employed between the remaining BRITISH COLONIES in NORTH AMERICA, and the BRITISH ISLANDS in WEST INDIES.

Number and tonnage of British vessels clearing outwards, and employed yearly in the trade between the remaining British colonies in North America, and the British islands in the West Indies, on an average of the years	Ships	Tons.
1770, 1771, and 1772, before the war .	15	753
Number and tonnage of ditto so employed, entering inwards, on a like average .	23	1,240
Medium of the average number and tonnage of British vessels, entering inwards, and clearing outwards......	19	996

	Ships	Tons.
Number and tonnage of British vessels, clearing outwards, and employed yearly in the trade between the remaining British colonies in North America, and the British islands in the West Indies, on an average of the years 1787, 1788, and 1789, since the war..	142	12,696
Number and tonnage of ditto so employed, entering inwards, on a like average.	171	16,331
Medium of the average number and tonnage of British vessels entering inwards, and clearing outwards	156	14,513

The account of the number of vessels from whence these averages are taken, includes their repeated voyages. The number of vessels so employed has increased since the war 137 ships, being seven times more than it was before the war: and the quantity of tonnage has increased 13,517 tons, being thirteen times more than it was before the war. Many of these vessels, before the war, belonged to the inhabitants of the countries which were then British colonies, but are now under the dominion of the United States they can now only belong to British subjects, resident in some part of His Majesty's present dominions.

As the result of the foregoing deduction the following table has been prepared, in which allowance is made for the repeated voyages, which the vessels employed in these different branches of trade are supposed to make in each year; and the number and tonnage of the vessels is reduced in due proportion. This table will shew, at one view, the increase and decrease of vessels and tonnage employed in these various branches of navigation; and how far the balance on the whole is at present in favour of Great-Britain

	Before the War.				Since the War.			
	Vessels, and their tonnage, belonging to merchants residing in the present British dominions; or to British merchants occasionally resident in the countries which were then British colonies, but now form the United States.		Vessels belonging to merchants, who were natives and permanent inhabitants of the countries which were then British colonies, but now form the United States.		Vessels belonging to the subjects of the present British dominions.		Vessels belonging to the subjects of the United States.	
	Vessels.	Tons.	Vessels.	Tons.	Vessels.	Tons.	Vessels.	Tons.
1st.—Vessels, and their tonnage, employed between Great Britain and the United States....	497	65,058	165	21,686	261	52,595	163	26,564
2d.—Vessels, and their tonnage, employed between Great Britain and the remaining British Colonies in North America....	228	9,816	32	1,402	367	46,106		
3d.—(a) Vessels, and their tonnage, employed between the remaining British colonies and the United States....	43	1,869	131	5,609	158	10,219		
4th.—(b) Vessels, and their tonnage, employed between the British islands in the West Indies and the United States....	93	4,489	651	31,423	181	20,912		
5th.—(c) Vessels, and their tonnage, employed between the remaining British colonies and the British islands in the West Indies....	1	83	4	249	52	4,837		
	862	81,315	983	60,369	1,019	134,669	163	26,564

(a) The number of vessels, and their tonnage, employed in this branch of freight, was divided by 1½, as it is estimated that these vessels make one voyage and a half in a year.

(b) The number of vessels in this branch of freight was divided by 3, as it is estimated that these vessels make three voyages in a year.

(c) The number of vessels, and their tonnage, employed in this branch of freight, was divided by 3, as it is estimated that these vessels also make three voyages in a year.

RECAPITULATION. Containing the increase and decrease under the forementioned different branches of freight, and the increase and decrease on the whole.

	BRITISH			AMERICAN	
	Vessels.	Tons.		Vessels.	Tons.
Increase on the 2d branch of freight .	139	36,289	Decrease on the 1st	2	
Increase on the 3d branch of freight	115	8,350	Decrease on the 2d. . .	32	1,402
Increase on the 4th branch of freight .	88	16,423	Decrease on the 3d..... .	131	5,609
Increase on the 5th branch of freight.. .	51	4,754	Decrease on the 4th .	651	31,423
			Decrease on the 5th ...	4	249
Total increase..	393	65,816	Total decrease	820	38,683
Decrease on the 1st branch of freight .	236	12,463	Increase on the 1st........	—	4,877
Balance of increase .	157	53,353	Balance of decrease	820	33,806

9.—An Account of the Tonnage of Vessels entered into the U₁
October, 1789, to the 30th of September 1790, distinguishi₁
of its Tonnage; and distinguishing the American from Fo

| STATES. | AMERICAN. | | | | EUROPE. | |
	Coasting Vessels.	Fishing Vessels.	Vessels in the Oversea Trade.	Total Tonnage.	Vessels belonging to Great Britain including Ireland.	Vessels belonging to other Nations.
Massachusetts ...	53,073	24,826	99,124	177,023	19,493	853
Pennsylvania	6,055	—	51,594	57,649	24,605	9,665
Virginia	9,914	55	33,560	43,529	56,273	4,092
Maryland	6,203	—	42,072	48,275	36,918	6,921
New York	16,099	60	39,272	55,431	23,339	9,485
* South Carolina..	508	—	16,871	17,379	18,725	4,256
† North Carolina .	5,723	—	24,219	29,942	4,941	244
Connecticut	6,330	—	24,286	30,616	2,556	—
Georgia	1,090	—	9,544	10,634	15,041	1,570
New Hampshire ..	1,670	473	11,376	13,519	3,458	34
‡ Rhode Island ..	1,626	838	7,061	9,525	95	221
Delaware	1,061	—	3,080	4,141	1,783	—
New Jersey	3,429	—	2,085	5,514	267	79
Total..	112,781	26,252	364,144	503,177	225,494	37,420

* In the Returns from Charles Town, one Quarter
† The Returns from this State did not commence
‡ The Returns from this State did not commence

Note.—This Table contains an account of the tonnage of vessels ente
period subsequent to any of those years on which the averages stated
all the tonnage belonging to the subjects of the United States of Ameri
their coasting trade, and their fisheries, which entered their ports durin₁
of it was employed in their foreign trade with the British dominions.
the preceding tables, is only of so much of the tonnage of the United
the various branches of commerce, with such parts of the British ₁
trade, in ships belonging to the said States. [177]

tates of AMERICA, from the 1st of
State according to the Magnitude
essels.

	RECAPITULATION.

	Total Tonnage of each Country.	
)9	Viz.	Tons.
9	United States	503,177
)4	Great Britain . 222,347	
4	Ireland 3,147½-225,494½	
;5	France 13,435½	
)0	Holland 8,815½	
:7	Spain . 8,551¼	
'2	Portugal . 2,924	
5	Denmark . . 1,619¾	
1	Germany ... 1,368	
1	Prussia 394	
.4	Sweden 311½- 37,419½	
)0		
)1	Total . .. 766,091	

ng, and not included.
1 of March, 1790.
of June, 1790.

several ports of the United States, in a
were formed. It contains an account of
oyed in every part of their foreign trade,
·riod; but does not distinguish what part
other hand, the account given above in
as was employed during those years in
1s with which they are allowed now to

Appendix, N° 2

10.–VALUE of EXPORTS from the UNITED STATES to different Parts of the World, from the Commencement of the Custom Houses in August, 1789, to 30th September, 1790, VIZ.

	Dollars.	Cents.*
Provisions	5,757,482	
Grain	2,519,232	
Fish	941,696	
Lumber	1,263,534	
Live stock	486,105	
	10,968,044	
Other articles	9,447,917	84

	Dollars.	Cents.
Total	20,415,966	84

Of these the Exports

	Dollars	Cents
To the Dominions of France.	4,698,735	: 48
D°. Great Britain	9,363,416	: 47
D°. Spain	2,005,907	· 16
D°. Portugal . . .	1,283,462	
D°. United Netherlands	1,963,880	: 9
D°. Denmark	224,415	: 50
D°. Sweden	47,240	
D°. Flanders.	14,298	
D°. Germany	487,787	: 14
D°. Mediterranean	41,298	
D°. African Coast and Islands	139,984	
D°. East Indies	135,181	
D°. North West Coast of America	10,362	
	20,415,966	: 84

Exclusive of many packages omitted in the returns from the custom-houses, which were exported from the United States.

* A cent is one hundredth part of a dollar, or about a halfpenny.

[179]

11.—LIST of such VESSELS (and the respective TONNAGE of each Denomination) as entered the Port of PHILADEL-PHIA, from the 1st Day of September 1772, to the 1st Day of September 1775, distinguishing each Year; and also distinguishing those which were owned in GREAT BRITAIN, IRELAND, and such Parts of the BRITISH Dominions as are not now comprehended within the UNITED STATES (N° 1); those which were owned in the Port of PHILADELPHIA alone (N° 2); and those which were owned in the Thirteen Colonies which now compose the UNITED STATES of AMERICA (N°. 3).

N° 1. BRITISH

1772 to 1773		1773 to 1774		1774 to 1775.	
N°.	Tons.	N°	Tons	N°	Tons.
23 Ships .	3,508	28 Ships	4,304	35 Ships . .	5,590
30 Brigantines	2,925	33 Brigantines	2,853	33 Brigantines .	3,170
4 Snows . . .	370	12 Snows	1,246	7 Snows .	730
22 Sloops .	1,043	24 Sloops	1,142	22 Sloops	1,006
18 Schooners .	822	22 Schooners	962	17 Schooners . .	842
97	8,668	119	10,507	114	11,338

N° 2. PHILADELPHIA

1772 to 1773.		1773 to 1774		1774 to 1775	
N°.	Tons	N°	Tons.	N°	Tons.
109 Ships	16,385	116 Ships. . . .	17,569	146 Ships	23,406
140 Brigantines .	12,148	176 Brigantines .	15,749	205 Brigantines .	17,802
25 Snows. . . .	2,902	18 Snows .	2,092	17 Snows	1,972
39 Sloops . .	1,806	42 Sloops .	1,844	36 Sloops .	1,844
63 Schooners .	3,226	54 Schooners .	2,959	35 Schooners . . .	1,834
376	36,467	406	40,213	439	46,858

N° 3 America.

1772 to 1773.		1773 to 1774		1774 to 1775.	
N°	Tons.	N°	Tons	N°	Tons.
5 Ships .	700	6 Ships	860	7 Ships ..	902
46 Brigantines .	3,856	28 Brigantines	2,224	30 Brigantines ..	2,576
1 Snow	160	.	. . .	1 Snow	80
139 Sloops	6,503	135 Sloops .	5,876	130 Sloops	5,843
80 Schooners .	3,899	81 Schooners	3,962	78 Schooners .	4,025
271	15,118	250	12,922	246	13,426

12.—A TABLE, shewing what Proportion the TONNAGE of GREAT BRITAIN employed out of the Port of PHILADEL-PHIA bore to the TONNAGE employed out of that Port, and owned therein, upon an Average of three Years antecedent to the War, and what Proportion the Tonnage of Great Britain so employed then bore to the Tonnage of Philadelphia, united with the Tonnage of the other twelve American Colonies so employed —Shewing also, what Proportion the British Tonnage now employed in the Trade of Philadelphia bears to the Tonnage of all the United States employed out of that Port, upon an Average of the last two Years.

	1773. Tons.	1774. Tons.	1775. Tons.	TOTAL Tons
British .	8,668	10,507	11,333	30,508
Philadelphia ..	36,467	40,213	46,858	123,538
American	15,118	12,922	13,426	41,466
Philadelphia and American combined.	51,585	53,135	60,284	165,004

By the foregoing table it appears, that the tonnage of Great Britain employed out of the port of Philadelphia in the above years was not equal to 1-4th part of the tonnage employed out of and owned in the port of Philadelphia;—

[181]

and that the tonnage of Great Britain then so employed, bore only a proportion as 2 does to 11 to the tonnage of Philadelphia and the other twelve colonies combined, so employed.

	1788. Tons	1789. Tons	TOTAL Tons.
British . . .	23,004	29,372	52,376
American .	28,028	37,728	65,756

By the above table it appears, that the tonnage of Great Britain employed out of the port of Philadelphia in the years 1788 and 1789, amounted to within one-fifth part of the tonnage of all the thirteen United States combined, so employed.

13.—A LIST of BRITISH VESSELS which entered the Port of Philadelphia the following Years, viz. from 5th September 1787, to 5th September 1788.

FROM GREAT BRITAIN		IRELAND		BRITISH WEST INDIES		BRITISH AMERICAN COLONIES	
Vessels	Tons	Vessels	Tons	Vessels	Tons	Vessels	Tons.
16 Ships .	3,748	4 Ships	1,021	1 Ship	174	1 Ship	160
19 Brigantines	2,907	1 Brig	135	52 Brigs	6,229	6 Brigantines	462
3 Snows .	456	1 Snow	90	64 Sloops .	5,597	1 Schooner	47
3 Sloops . . .	198			24 Schooners	1,695		
1 Schooner .	85						
42 Sail.	7,394	6 Sail	1,246	141 Sail.	13,695	8 Sail.	669

TOTAL.
22 Ships .
78 Brigantines .
4 Snows . ⎫
67 Sloops . ⎬ 197 Sail Vessels — 23,004 Tons
26 Schooners . ⎭

Appendix, N° 2

A LIST of BRITISH VESSELS which entered the Port of Philadelphia the following Years, viz. from 5th September 1788, to 5th September 1789.

FROM GREAT BRITAIN.		IRELAND		BRITISH WEST INDIES.		BRITISH AMERICAN COLONIES.	
Vessels	Tons	Vessels	Tons.	Vessels.	Tons.	Vessels.	Tons.
23 Ships ..	5,967	15 Ships	2,961	3 Ships	600	1 Ship ..	162
19 Brigantines	2,936	5 Brigantines	631	48 Brigantines	6,010	10 Brigantines	1,060
1 Snow . .	104	1 Snow. .	108	69 Sloops .	5,586	2 Sloops ...	106
4 Sloops . .	223			29 Schooners	2,332	7 Schooners	544
1 Schooner ..	42						
48 Sail.	9,272	21 Sail.	3,700	149 Sail	14,528	20 Sail	1,872

TOTAL

42 Ships . .	
82 Brigantines . ..	
2 Snows. . . .	238 Sail Vessels — 29,372 Tons.
75 Sloops. . . .	
37 Schooners. .	

14.—Account of Vessels belonging to other European Nations, which entered the principal Ports of the United States in the following Years; viz.

1787.   Charles Town.

	Ships.	Brigantines	Schooners.	Sloops.	American Tonnage.
Spain	0	2	39	3	1,073
France	0	4	2	2	715
United Netherlands	1	4	0	0	799
Altona	1	0	0	0	280
Bremen	0	1	0	0	193
Denmark . .	0	1	0	0	164
Hamburgh	0	1	0	0	130
Austria	0	1	0	0	127
	2	14	41	5	3,481

1788.	Philadelphia.				
France	1	4	1	0	692
Holland	0	4	4	2	1,022
Spain	7	6	4	0	2,335
Portugal	0	3	0	0	321
Sweden	0	2	0	1	430
Denmark	0	1	0	0	157
Prussia	0	2	0	0	388
	8	22	9	3	5,345

Appendix, N° 2

	Ships.	Brigantines	Schooners.	Sloops	American Tonnage.
France............ ...	1	5	0	0	1,000
Holland.	2	1	0	0	960
Spain	3	3	1	4	1,580
Portugal	3	4	1	0	1,380
Sweden	0	2	0	0	400
	9	15	2	4	5,320

1789.

Supposed from the best information
{
To Virginia.	2,664
Maryland..	2,348
North Carolina	3,000
Georgia	2,500
Massachusetts	1,758

	26,416
Add to the above amount one-fourth for the rest of theUnited States... . .	6,604
Total amount	33,020

Which is little more than one-fourth of the tonnage of the vessels belonging to British merchants in all the different branches of this commerce, not allowing, in either case, for repeated voyages.

It is left to the intelligent reader to draw his own conclusions from the above tables and statements; and, in addition to what has been said, I shall only further observe, that the total annual decrease in value, since the war, of British manufactures and other articles, exported from Great Britain to the countries belonging to the United States, has amounted to ....£. 398,393

> The total annual increase in value, since the
> war, of the like articles, exported from Great
> Britain, to the remaining British colonies
> in North America, has been   449,677
> To the British West Indian islands 114,801
> Total.   .... .564,478

So that upon the whole the annual increase in value, since the war, of British manufactures and other articles exported from Great Britain to North America and the West Indies, has amounted to .. . . £. 166,085

> The total annual decrease in value, since the
> war, of import in to Great Britain from
> the United States, has amounted to   . £. 843,506

> The total annual increase in value, since the
> war, of imports into Great Britain from
> the remaining British colonies in North
> America, has been   ...   . £. 96,986
> From the British West Indian islands. 671,066
> Total.... . ....£. 768,052

So that upon the balance total, the decrease has been.......   75,454

This decrease has been chiefly owing to the decreased

importation of tobacco and rice (the Americans not being any longer obliged to ship their produce for British ports only) amounting in value,

Upon 44,774,458 lbs. of the former, to........£. 582,987
Upon 259,035 cwt. of the latter, to.   .   . .   196,526
In the whole to.....   . . .. £. 779,513

The value of exports to the countries now belonging to the United States, has exceeded the value of imports from thence, without including Ireland, in a much greater proportion since the war than before it, the balance of trade, therefore, is more in favour of Great Britain.

It must be highly satisfactory to the reader to know, that the value of the British exports of 1789 exceeded those of 1784, to all countries, by.. ....£. 4,400,609

N. B.—The reader may possibly discover two or three trifling inaccuracies, none of them, however, (if there are any such) exceeding a fraction, or at most an unit, in the preceding computations; which the Editor has not thought it necessary to notice.

15.—AN ACCOUNT of the Number of Ships and Brigs built in the Ports of the UNITED STATES, in the Year 1772, compared with the like Vessels building in the said States in 1789.*

STATES.	1772.		1789.	
	Vessels.	Tons.	Vessels.	Tons.
New Hampshire	—	—	6	—
Massachusetts	—	—	5	—
Rhode Island	—	—	—	—
Connecticut	—	—	—	—
Total of the N. England Provinces	123	18,149	11	0
New York	15	1,640	—	—
New Jersey	1	80	1	200
Pennsylvania	18	2,897	14	2,966
Maryland	8	1,626	5	1,200
Virginia	7	933	—	—
North Carolina	3	253	—	—
South Carolina	2	213	—	—
Georgia	5	753	—	—
Total	182		31	

* In the account of ships and brigs built in the ports of the United States in the year 1772, there is no specification of the numbers built in each of the New England provinces, but a total only of the number and tonnage of vessels built in all these provinces; nor was any account given of the tonnage of the eleven vessels building in the provinces of New Hampshire and Massachusetts Bay in 1789. So that it is not possible to make a comparison of the quantity of tonnage of which the vessels in the foregoing table consists.

APPENDIX, N° 3.

THE success of this institution has in no degree corresponded to the excellence of the design. The aboriginal Indians are from their infancy accustomed to an idle and roving life; they are chiefly employed in hunting, fowling, or fishing, or, as soon as they are able to carry arms or a tomahawk, to war; and it is almost impossible to reclaim them from this savage and dissipated mode of life. Not many years ago, a remarkable instance happened at Williamsburg, which greatly exemplifies the present observation: The Cherokees had with difficulty been prevailed upon to suffer one of their children, a youth of nine or ten years of age, to be conducted to Williamsburg, in order that he might be educated in Mr. Boyle's school. The young Indian soon shewed himself impatient of restraint and confinement; he grew sullen, would learn nothing, and although every means were tried to please him (for it was the wish and interest of the colony that he should be pleased) appeared always dissatisfied and unhappy. One morning he was missed, and although every possible inquiry was made, no tidings could be heard, nor the least information received concerning him: he had not been seen by any one, either planter or negro; and as the distance of the Cherokee country was four or five hundred miles, separated by large rivers abounding with sharks, or immense forests full of venomous serpents or wild beasts, it was justly apprehended that he must inevitably perish; and as it would be impossible

[189]

to convince the Indians of the real truth of the case, it might unhappily occasion a war with the Cherokee nation, a circumstance of the most calamitous importance. It fortunately happened, however, that the young Indian got safe home, he headed or swam over the great rivers that obstructed his way; concealed himself in the woods during the day, travelled in the night, supported himself with the tuckahoe and other roots and berries, and by that natural sagacity which is characteristic of the Indians * explored his way through an immense extent of trackless woods and forests to his native cabin. At present the only Indian children in Mr. Boyle's school are five or six of the Pamunky tribe, who, being surrounded by and living in the midst of our settlements, are more accustomed to the manners and habits of the English colonists.

A circumstance similar to the above I find mentioned by Mr. Catesby in his Natural History of Carolina; and it probably refers to the same event. The story, as I have related it, was communicated to 'me by the Hon and Rev. Mr. Commissary Dawson, President of the College.

The character of the North American Indians is not to be collected from observations upon the Pamunky, or any other Indian tribe living within the boundaries of the British settlements. These are in many respects changed, per-

---

* A melancholy proof of the inferiority of Europeans to Indians in this respect happened in the year 1757, when Col. Spotswood, who was out with a party of rangers formed of Virginia gentlemen, for the protection of the frontiers, unfortunately strayed from his companions, could not find his way back either to them, or to any of our settlements, though constantly used to be out upon hunting-parties, and miserably perished in the woods.

haps not for the better, from their original customs and moral habits. In general the North American Indians resemble each other in the great outlines and features of character, but intercourse with the Europeans, excessive use of brandy and other spirits, and, which is almost irresistible, the depravity and immoral example of our Indian traders and back-settlers, all these have concurred in a most unfortunate degree to corrupt and contaminate their minds. It is not my intention to enter into a discussion of this subject, but the following anecdotes, for the truth of which I can answer, may possibly cast some light upon it, and may occasionally be of use to any future historian, who shall undertake to consider and treat of it more largely.

Previous to my arrival in Virginia, a war had been upon the point of breaking out between the Nottoway and a tribe of the Tuscarora Indians, on account of a murder that had been committed upon the former by one of the latter nation; they were both of them in alliance with the English, and as the war raged at that time with incredible fury upon the frontiers, it was of great moment to prevent a rupture, and, if possible, to reconcile the differences between them. For this purpose frequent conferences had been held by the Lieutenant Governor of Virginia with the chiefs of the Nottoway nation, and several talks and negotiations had passed between them. The business was not entirely concluded when I arrived at Williamsburg; and very soon after a party of Indians arrived from the Nottoway country, which borders upon North Carolina, on the same errand. Amongst those who composed the train was a warrior, named Captain Charles; and as he was the principal personage entrusted by his nation with the commission, I endeavoured to form an acquaintance with him, and to insinuate myself into his good opinion; with this view I invited him to my apartment, and by showing him some little civility I so far succeeded, that he expressed himself sensible of my attention, and promised when he next came to Williamsburg, which, he said, if his nation approved of his mission, he should do very shortly, he would bring me some present as a token of his acknowledgment and remembrance. Accordingly some time after, walking in the streets of Williamsburg, I accidentally met him; and after accosting and saluting him in the usual manner, by giving him my hand, and making a few enquiries, I said, "Well, Cap-"tain Charles, where is the present you promised me?"— He immediately hung down his head, and said, "I have "forgot it"—I inconsiderately replied, "It does not much "signify, but I thought an Indian never forgot his promise." After this we separated, and I thought no more of the transaction; but in the afternoon information was brought to the Lieutenant Governor, that the Indians had suddenly disappeared, without having received the presents intended for them by government; and that it was feared they had gone away in disgust, and that the negotiation would have an unfortunate issue. Two or three days passed under these alarming circumstances. At length, however, they returned, increased in number, and generally laden with presents, or curiosities intended for sale. It then appeared that Captain Charles, stung with my reproach, had gone back to the Nottoway country; or, which is more likely, as he was absent only two or three days, into the swamps or woods, to fetch the articles which he had promised me.

The other anecdote is of a much more interesting and more striking nature. About the year 1756, Col. Peter Randolph, Col. Byrd, Mr. Campbell, and other persons, were sent upon an embassy by the Governor of Virginia to the Cherokee country, in order, if possible, to cement more strongly the friendship and alliance which subsisted at that time between our colonies and those savages, and to engage them more heartily in our cause. The business was in train, and likely to succeed, when unfortunately the following most flagrant and atrocious act of treachery immediately put an end to the negotiation, and eventually involved us in a new and bloody war with the very nation whose friendship and aid it was the object of the mission to cement and make more firm and lasting. The reader should be informed, that the cruel depredations and ravages committed by the Indians after General Braddock's defeat, had induced government to offer a considerable premium for every scalp of a hostile Indian, that should be brought in by any of our rangers. this unfortunately opened a door, and gave occasion to many acts of enormity; for some of the back-settlers, men of bad lives and worse principles, tempted by the reward, insidiously massacred several of our friendly Indians, and afterwards endeavoured to defraud government of the reward, by pretending that they were the scalps of hostile tribes. Amongst others, a back-settler in Augusta county, a captain of militia, whose name ought to be delivered down to posterity with infamy, treacherously murdered some Cherokee Indians, who had been out upon a military expedition in our behalf against the French, under a pretence that they had pilfered some of his poultry. He had received and entertained them as friends; and when they took leave of him to return to their own country, he placed a party in ambush, murdered several of the poor unsuspecting Cherokees, and then endeavoured to defraud government, by claiming the premium assigned for the scalps of hostile Indians. A few of those who escaped the massacre arrived at the Cherokee town with the news of this horrid transaction, just at the moment when the embassy was upon the point of concluding a very advantageous treaty: a violent ferment immediately took place, and the Cherokees, in the utmost rage, assembled from every quarter, to take instant revenge by putting all the embassadors to death.

Attakulla Kulla, or the Little Carpenter, a steady friend of the English, hastened to the ambassadors, apprised them of their danger, and recommended to them to conceal or barricade themselves as well as they could, and not to appear abroad on any account. He then assembled his nation, over whom he possessed great influence, in the councilroom; inveighed bitterly against the treachery of the English, advised an immediate war to revenge the injury; and never to lay down the hatchet, till they had obtained full compensation and atonement for the blood of their countrymen. "Let us not, however," said he, "violate our faith, "or the laws of hospitality, by imbruing our hands in the "blood of those who are now in our power; they came to "us in the confidence of friendship, with belts of wampum "to cement a perpetual alliance with us. Let us carry "them back to their own settlements; conduct them safely "within their confines; and then take up the hatchet, and "endeavour to exterminate the whole race of them." They accordingly adopted this counsel; they conducted the ambassadors safe to the confines; and as they could not obtain satisfaction for the murder, by having the offender delivered up to them, which they demanded, and which ought to have been done, a dreadful war ensued, in which the different tribes of the Cherokee nation became gradually involved; and which did not cease, or relax from its horrors, till terminated by Col. Grant in the year 1761, with still more horrid circumstances than any that had been exercised during the carrying of it on.

This account was communicated to me by one of the gentlemen engaged in the embassy.

Mr. Jefferson, in his History of Virginia, page 99, has related the following circumstance, that occurred during this awful and interesting transaction. Speaking of the strict observance and fidelity of Indians in regard to their promises and attachments, he says, in a note: "A remark-"able instance of this, appeared in the case of the late Col. "Byrd, who was sent to the Cherokee nation to transact "some business with them. It happened that some of our "disorderly people had killed one or two of that nation; "it was therefore proposed in council that Col. Byrd "should be put to death, in revenge for the loss of their "countrymen. Among them was a chief called Silouèe, "who on some former occasion had contracted an acquaint-"ance and friendship with Col. Byrd; he came to him every "night in his tent, and told him not to be afraid, they should "not kill him. After many days deliberation, however, "the determination was, contrary to Silouèe's expectation, "that Byrd should be put to death, and some warriors were

"dispatched as executioners. Silouèe attended them, and
"when they entered the tent, he threw himself between
"them and Byrd, and said to the warriors, *This man is my*
"*friend, before you get at him you must kill me:*—on which
"they returned, and the council respected the principle so
" much as to recede from their determination."

APPENDIX, N° 4.

THOMAS LORD FAIRFAX, descended from a very ancient family in Yorkshire, was born towards the latter end of the last century, I believe about the year 1691. He was the eldest son of Thomas fifth Lord Fairfax, of Cameron, in the kingdom of Scotland, by Catherine, only daughter and heiress of Thomas Lord Culpepper; in whose right he afterwards possessed Leeds Castle, with several manors and estates in the county of Kent, and in the Isle of Wight, and that immense tract of country, comprised within the boundaries of the rivers Potowmac and Rappahannoc in Virginia, called the Northern Neck, containing by estimation five millions seven hundred thousand acres.

Lord Fairfax had the misfortune to lose his father while young: and at his decease he and his two brothers, Henry and Robert, and four sisters, one of whom, named Frances, was afterwards married to Denny Martin, Esq., of Loose, in Kent, came under the guardianship of their mother and grandmother, the dowager Ladies Fairfax and Culpepper; the latter of whom was a princess of the house of Hesse Cassel.

Lord Fairfax, at the usual age, was sent to the university of Oxford to complete his education, and was highly esteemed there for his learning and accomplishments. His judgment upon literary subjects was then, and at other times, frequently appealed to; and he was one of the writers of that incomparable work, the Spectator. After some years residence in the university, he took a commission in the regiment of horse, called the Blues, and remained in it, I believe, till the death of the survivor of the two ladies above mentioned; who had usually resided at Leeds Castle. Some time before their decease, a circumstance happened, that eventually occasioned him much serious chagrin and uneasiness. He had been persuaded, upon his brother Henry's arriving at the age of twenty-one years, or rather compelled by the ladies Culpepper and Fairfax, under a menace, in case of refusal, of never inheriting the Northern Neck, to cut off the entail, and to sell Denton Hall, and the Yorkshire estates, belonging to this branch of the Fairfax family, which had been in their possession for five or six centuries, in order to redeem those of the late Lord Culpepper, that had descended to his heiress, exceedingly encumbered, and deeply mortgaged. This circumstance happened while Lord Fairfax was at Oxford, and is said to have occasioned him the greater vexation, as it appeared afterwards, that the estates had been disposed of, through the treachery of a steward, for considerably less than their value; less even than what the timber that was cut down to discharge the purchase money, before the stipulated day of payment came, was sold for. He conceived a violent disgust against the ladies, who, as he used to say, had treated him with such unparalleled cruelty; and ever afterwards expressed the keenest sense of the injury that had been done, as he thought, to the Fairfax family. After entering into possession, he began to inquire into the value and situation of his estates; and he soon discovered that the proprietary lands in Virginia, had been extremely mismanaged and under-let. An agent, who at the same time was a tenant, had been employed by the dowager Lady Fairfax, to superintend her concerns in that quarter of the world; and he is said to have abused her confidence, and to have enriched himself and family, as is too frequently the case, at the expense of his employer. Lord Fairfax therefore wrote to William Fairfax, Esq., his father's brother's second son, who held, at that time, a place of considerable trust and emolument under government in New England; requesting him to remove to Virginia, and to take upon himself the agency of the Northern Neck. With this request Mr. Fairfax readily complied; and, as soon as he conveniently could, he removed with his family to Virginia, and settled in Westmoreland county. He there opened an agency office for the granting of the proprietary lands; and as the quit-rent demanded was only after the rate of two shillings for every hundred acres, the vacant lands were rapidly let, and a considerable and permanent income was soon derived from them. Lord Fairfax, informed of these circumstances, determined to go himself to Virginia, to visit his estates, and the friend and relation to whom he was so greatly obliged. Accordingly, about the year 1739, he embarked for that continent; and on his arrival in Virginia, he went and spent twelve months with his friend Mr. Fairfax, at his house in Westmoreland county; during which time he became so captivated with the climate, the beauties and produce of the country, that he formed a resolution of returning to England, in order to prosecute a suit, which he had with the Crown, on account of a considerable tract of land claimed in behalf of the latter by Governor Gooch; (which suit was afterwards determined in his favour;) and, after making some necessary arrangements, and settling his family affairs, to return to Virginia, and spend the remainder of his life upon his vast and noble domain there. I am not certain in what year this happened, or how long Lord Fairfax remained in England. He was present at his brother Robert's first marriage, which, according to Mr. Hasted, [see Hist. of Kent, vol II page 478] took place in the year 1741; for he frequently mentioned the fatigue he underwent in sitting up for a month together, full dressed and in form to receive visits upon that occasion: nor did he go back to Virginia before the year 1745, because, when he arrived there, Mr. William Fairfax had removed out of Westmoreland into Fairfax county, to a beautiful house which he had built upon the banks of the Potowmac, a little below Mount Vernon, called Belvoir, which he did not do previous to that time. In all probability therefore, Lord Fairfax first went to America about the year 1739, returned to England the year following, and finally settled in the Northern Neck in 1746, or 1747. On his return he went to Belvoir, the seat of his friend and relation Mr William Fairfax, and remained several years in his family, undertaking and directing the management of his farms and plantations, and amusing himself with hunting, and the pleasures of the field. At length, the lands about Belvoir not answering his expectation, and the foxes becoming less numerous, he determined to remove to a fine tract of land on the western side of the Blue Ridge, or Apalachian mountains, in Frederic county, about eighty miles from Belvoir; where he built a small neat house, which he called Greenway Court; and laid out one of the most beautiful farms, consisting of arable and grazing lands, and of meadows two or three miles in length, that had ever been seen in that quarter of the world. He there lived the remainder of his life, in the style of a gentleman farmer; or, I should rather have said, of an English country gentleman. He kept many servants, white and black; several hunters; a plentiful but plain table, entirely in the English fashion; and his mansion was the mansion of hospitality. His dress corresponded with his mode of life, and, notwithstanding he had every year new suits of clothes, of the most fashionable and expensive kind, sent out to him from England, which he never put on, was plain in the extreme. His manners were humble, modest, and unaffected; not tinctured in the smallest degree with arrogance, pride, or self-conceit. He was free from the selfish passions, and liberal almost to excess. The produce of his farms, after the deduction of what was necessary for the consumption of his own family, was distributed and given away to the poor planters and settlers in his neighborhood. To these he frequently advanced money, to enable them to go on with their improvements; to clear away the woods, and cultivate the ground, and where the lands proved unfavourable, and not likely to answer the labour and expectation of the planter or husbandman, he usually indemnified him for the expense he had been at in the attempt, and gratuitously granted him fresh lands of a more favourable and promising nature. He was a friend and a father to all who held and lived under him; and as the great object of his ambition was the peopling and cultivating of that fine and beautiful country, of which he was the proprietor, he sacrificed every other pursuit, and made every other consideration subordinate, to this great point.

Lord Fairfax had been brought up in revolution principles, and had early imbibed high notions of liberty, and of the excellence of the British constitution. He devoted a considerable part of his time to the public service. He was Lord Lieutenant and Custos Rotulorum of the county of Frederic, presided at the county courts held at Winchester, where during the sessions he always kept open table; and acted as surveyor and overseer of the highways and public roads. His chief if not sole amusement was hunting; and in pursuit of this exercise he frequently carried his hounds to distant parts of the country; and entertained every gentleman of good character and decent appearance, who attended him in the field, at the inn or ordinary, where he took up his residence for the hunting season. So unexceptionable and disinterested was his behaviour, both public and private, and so generally was he beloved and respected, that during the late contest between Great Britain and America, he never met with the least insult or molestation from either party, but was suffered to go on in his improvement and cultivation of the Northern Neck, a pursuit equally calculated for the comfort and happiness of individuals, and for the general good of mankind.

In the year 1751, Thomas Martin, Esq., second son of his sister Frances, came over to Virginia to live with his lordship, and a circumstance happened, a few years after his arrival, too characteristic of Lord Fairfax not to be recorded. After General Braddock's defeat in the year 1755, the Indians in the interest of the French, committed the most dreadful massacres upon all our back settlements. Their incursions were everywhere stained with blood, and slaughter and devastation marked the inroads of these cruel and merciless savages. Every planter of name or reputation became an object of their insidious designs; and as Lord Fairfax had been pointed out to them as a captain or chief of great renown, the possession of his scalp became an object of their sanguinary ambition, and what they would have regarded as a trophy of inestimable value With this view they made daily inroads into the vicinage of Greenway Court; and it is said, that not less than 3,000 lives fell sacrifices to their cruel barbarity between the Appalachian and Allegheny mountains.* The most serious apprehensions were entertained for the safety of Lord Fairfax and the family at Greenway Court. In this crisis of danger his lordship, importuned by his friends and the principal gentry of the colony to retire to the inner settlements for security, is said to have addressed his nephew, who now bore the commission of colonel of militia, nearly in the following

* It was at this crisis that the gentlemen of Virginia associated themselves under the command of Peyton Randolph, Esq., afterwards President of the first Congress, for the protection of the frontiers The dismay occasioned by the ravages of the Indians was indescribable. Upon one day in particular an universal panic ran like wildfire through every part of Virginia, rumour reporting that the Indians had passed the mountains, were entering Williamsburg, and indeed every other town at the same moment, had scalped all who came in their way, and that nothing but immediate flight could save the wretched inhabitants from destruction All was hurry and confusion, every one endeavouring to escape death by flying from his own to some other town or plantation, where the alarm and consternation were equally great. At length certain information was brought, that the Indians were still beyond the mountains at least 150 miles off· and then, every one began to wonder, as they did in London after the panic during the rebellion of 1745, how it was possible that such an alarm could have arisen; or whence it could have originated.

manner:—"Colonel Martin, the danger we are exposed to,
"which is undoubtedly great, may possibly excite in your
"mind apprehension and anxiety. If so, I am ready to
"take any step that you may judge expedient for our com-
"mon safety. I myself am an old man, and it is of little
"importance whether I fall by the tomahawk of an Indian
"or by disease and old age. but you are young, and, it is to
"be hoped, may have many years before you. I will there-
"fore submit it to your decision, whether we shall remain
"where we are, taking every precaution to secure ourselves
"against the outrages of the enemy, or abandon our habi-
"tation and retire within the mountains, that we may be
"sheltered from the danger to which we are at present
"exposed. If we determine to remain, it is possible, not-
"withstanding our utmost care and vigilance, that we may
"both fall victims; if we retire, the whole district will im-
"mediately break up; and all the trouble and solicitude
"which I have undergone to settle this fine country will be
"frustrated, and the occasion perhaps irrecoverably lost."
Colonel Martin, after a short deliberation, determined to
remain, and as our affairs in that quarter soon took a more
favourable turn, and measures were adopted by government for securing our settlements against the carnage and
depredation of the Indians, the danger gradually diminished,
and at length entirely disappeared. From that time to the
present little or no molestation has been given to the back
settlements of the Northern Neck, extending from the
Appalachian to the Allegheny mountains.

Lord Fairfax, though possessed of innumerable good
qualities, had some few singularities in his character, that
occasionally exposed him to the smiles of the ignorant: but

they resembled the solar spots, which can scarcely be said to diminish the splendor of that bright luminary upon whose disk they appear. Early in life he had formed an attachment to a young lady of quality; and matters had proceeded so far, as to induce him to provide carriages, clothes, servants, and other necessary appendages for such an occasion Unfortunately, or rather let me say fortunately, before the contract was sealed, a more advantageous or dazzling offer was made to the lady, who thought herself at liberty to accept it; and she preferred the higher honour of being a duchess to the inferior station of a baroness. This disappointment is thought to have made a deep impression upon Lord Fairfax's mind; and to have had no inconsiderable share in determining him to retire from the world, and to settle in the wild and at that time almost uninhabited forests of North America. It is thought also to have excited in him a general dislike of the sex; in whose company, unless he was particularly acquainted with the parties, it is said he was reserved and under evident constraint and embarrassment. But I was present, when, upon a visit of ceremony to Lieutenant Governor Fauquier, who had lately arrived from England, he was introduced to his lady, and nothing of the kind appeared to justify the observation He remained at the palace three or four days; and during that time his behaviour was courteous, polite, and becoming a man of fashion. He possibly might not entertain a very favourable opinion of the sex; owing partly to the above mentioned circumstance, and partly to the treatment he had experienced from the ladies of Leeds Castle; but this does not seem to have influenced his general behaviour in regard to them. He had lived many years retired from the world, in a remote wilderness, sequestered from all polished society; and perhaps might not feel himself perfectly at ease, when he came into large parties of ladies, where ceremony and form were to be observed; but he had not forgot those accomplished manners which he had acquired in his early youth, at Leeds Castle, at the university, and in the army. His motive for settling in America was of the most noble and heroic kind. It was, as he always himself declared, to settle and cultivate that beautiful and immense tract of country, of which he was the proprietor, and in this he succeeded beyond his most sanguine expectations, for the Northern Neck was better peopled, better cultivated, and more improved, than any other part of the dominion of Virginia. Lord Fairfax lived to extreme old age at Greenway Court, universally beloved, and died as universally lamented, in January or February 1782, in the 92d year of his age. He was buried I believe at Winchester, where he had so often and so honourably presided as judge of the court. He bequeathed Greenway Court to his nephew Colonel Martin, who has since constantly resided there; and his barony descended to his only surviving brother Robert Fairfax, to whom he had before consigned Leeds Castle, and his other English estates.

Robert, seventh Lord Fairfax, died at Leeds Castle in 1791, and bequeathed that noble mansion, and its appendages, to his nephew the reverend Denny Martin, who has since taken the name of Fairfax, and is still living.

The barony or title by regular descent is vested in Brian Fairfax, third son of William Fairfax above mentioned, who lives in Virginia; and of whom more will be said in the sequel.

Appendix, N° 4

Having so frequently mentioned William Fairfax, Esquire, who came from New England, to take upon himself the agency of the Northern Neck, it may not be unacceptable to the reader, to learn something of the history of that worthy and respectable gentleman; and of the several branches of the Fairfax family descended from him, who are now settled in Virginia. William Fairfax, was the second son of the honourable Henry Fairfax of Towlston Hall, in Yorkshire. This gentleman's father Henry, fourth Lord Fairfax, left, besides other children, two sons, viz. Thomas, who succeeded him in the barony, and who married the heiress of the Culpepper family, and Henry, father of William, of whom I am now speaking. William, his father dying while he was young, was educated under the auspices of his uncle and godfather, the good Lord Lonsdale, at Lowther school, in Westmoreland; where he acquired a competent knowledge, not only of the classics, but of the modern languages. At the age of twenty-one he entered into the army, and served in Spain during Queen Anne's war, under his uncle Colonel Martin Bladen, to whom he was also secretary. At the conclusion of that war, he was prevailed upon to accompany captain Fairfax of the navy, who was also his relation, and other godfather, to the East Indies; but the sea not agreeing with him, he at his return took a second commission in the army, and went upon the expedition against the Island of Providence, at that time in possession of pirates. After the reduction of the island, he was appointed governor of it, and he there married, March the 27th, 1723-4, Sarah, daughter of Major Thomas Walker, who, with his family had accompanied the expedition, and was afterwards appointed chief justice of the Bahama Islands. By this lady he had a son, born the 2d of January following, whom he named George William. His health suffering extremely at this place, from the intense heat of the climate, he applied to government for an appointment in New England, and he had removed to that country, and was there resident, when solicited by Lord Fairfax, to take upon himself the agency of the Northern Neck. During his abode in New England, he had the misfortune to lose his lady, by whom he had two sons and two daughters: George William, mentioned above, who was born in the Island of Providence, and Thomas, Anne and Sarah, born in New England.

Mrs. Fairfax, upon her death-bed, requested her husband, after her decease, to marry a Miss Deborah Clarke of Salem, a lady of uncommon understanding, and her most intimate friend; from a conviction, which appeared to be well founded, that she would prove a kind step-mother, and faithful guardian to her orphan children. Accordingly Mr. Fairfax, in compliance with this request, some little time before he removed to Virginia, espoused this lady, and by her had three other children, viz two sons and a daughter, named Brian, William, and Hannah; so that he had in the whole seven children, four sons and three daughters, most of whom survived him. He departed this life at Belvoir, the 3d day of September 1757, aged sixty-six years. Mr. William Fairfax was a gentleman of very fine accomplishments, and general good character He was a kind husband, an indulgent parent, a faithful friend, a sincere Christian; and was eminently distinguished for his private and public virtues. Through the interest of two of his relations, Brian and Ferdinando Fairfax, who lived in London, and of whom the former was a commissioner of the excise, he had been appointed Lord Lieutenant and Custos Rotulorum of the county of Fairfax, collector of the customs of South Potomac, and one of his majesty's council, of which, in process of time, he became president, and continued in that honourable station many years. He was succeeded in his estate and employments by his eldest son, George William Fairfax. George William, at an early age, had been sent to England for education, and had been brought up in the same principles which had been professed by Lord Fairfax, and the rest of the family. At his return to Virginia, he married Sarah, daughter of Colonel Cary, of Hampton, upon James river, of the family of Hunsdon; and usually resided at his beautiful place at Belvoir, except during the sessions of the assembly and of the general courts, when his duty, as one of his majesty's council, obliged him to be at Williamsburg.

In the year 1773, some estates in Yorkshire having devolved to him by the death of Henry, his father's elder brother, he found it necessary to go to England to take possession of them. So critical was his arrival, that he passed in the river Thames the ill-omened tea, which eventually occasioned the separation of the American colonies from the mother-country. During the ten years contest, the consequences of which Mr. Fairfax early foresaw and lamented, his estates in Virginia were sequestered, and he received no remittances from his extensive property in that quarter of the world. This induced him to remove out of Yorkshire, from a house which he had recently furnished, to lay down his carriages, and to retire to Bath, where he lived in a private but genteel manner; and confined his expenses so much within the income of his English estates, that he was able occasionally to send large sums to the government agent, for the use and benefit of the American prisoners. He died at Bath, generally lamented on account of his many virtues and accomplishments, on the 3d of April 1787, in the sixty-third year of his age; and was buried in Writhlington church, in the county of Somerset, a few miles distant from that city. He left a widow, a very amiable lady, of distinguished merit, in great affluence; who has ever since resided in Bath Having no issue, he bequeathed his Virginia estates to Ferdinando, the second son of his half-brother Brian, the present Lord Fairfax.

Thomas, second son of William Fairfax, by Sarah Walker, and own brother to the above, entered into the navy; and was killed in an action in the East Indies on the 26th of June 1746. He was esteemed one of the handsomest men of his age. The following inscription to his memory was written by his disconsolate father, a few hours after he had received the melancholy account of his death:

"To the memory of Mr. Thomas Fairfax, second son of
"William Fairfax, Esquire, who died, fighting in his coun-
"try's cause, on board the Harwich ship of war, in an en-
"gagement with Monsieur Bourdenaye, commander of a
"French squadron on the Indian coast, the 26th day of
"June 1746, and in the twenty-first year of his age, beloved
"of his commander, Captain Carteret, and highly favoured
"by his friend Commodore Barnet, for his politeness of
"manners. He was a comely personage; of undoubted
"bravery; skilled in the theory of the profession; excelled
"by few as a naval draughtsman, and gave early promises,
"by a pregnant genius and diligent application, of a con-

"summate officer for the service of his country. But the "wisdom of Heaven is inscrutable human life is ever in "the hands of its author and while the good and brave are "always ready for death, resignation becomes their sur-"viving friends. Convinced of this duty, yet subdued by "the sentiments of a tender parent, this tablet was inscribed "and dedicated by his sorrowful father.

"May, Britain, all thy sons like him behave;
"Like him be virtuous, and like him be brave:
"Thy fiercest foes undaunted he withstood,
"And perish'd fighting for his country's good."

Anne, eldest daughter of William Fairfax, by Sarah Walker, was married to Lawrence, elder brother of Colonel, now General Washington. Lawrence, who had been educated in England, was a captain in the army, and possessed a very considerable landed property in Virginia. An infant daughter was the only fruit of this marriage, who died under seven years of age. At her decease, her father being also dead, General Washington succeeded to Mount Vernon, and several fine Virginian estates, the property of this branch of the Washington family. Anne, after the death of Lawrence Washington her husband, married George Lee, Esquire, the head of that numerous family in Virginia; and left behind her three sons, who are now living, viz. George Fairfax Lee, Launcelot Lee, and William Lee.

Sarah, second daughter of William Fairfax by Sarah Walker, was married to Mr. Carlyle, a merchant of Alexandria, in Fairfax county, and left two daughters; the eldest married to Mr Herbert, a merchant of the same place; the younger to Mr. Whiteing, a private gentleman of good fortune. Mrs. Whiteing died in childbed of her first child, a son, who is now living.

Brian, eldest son of the second marriage of William Fairfax with Deborah Clarke, the present and eighth baron, married Elizabeth, youngest daughter of Wilson Cary, Esquire, of the family above mentioned, and lives upon his estate at a place called Towlston, in Fairfax county. He has, by this marriage, two sons, viz. Thomas and Ferdinando, and one daughter, named Elizabeth, married to Mr. Griffith, the son of an American bishop. He has also a daughter by a second marriage. Thomas has been twice married, but has had the misfortune to lose both his wives, precisely at the same period of time, viz. the end of three months, by sickness and other indisposition, attendant upon pregnancy. Ferdinando, heir, as was above mentioned, to George William Fairfax, married a daughter of Wilson Miles Cary, Esquire, brother to the widow of the said George William, which marriage made the fifth connection between the families of Fairfax and Cary, either in England or Virginia.

William Fairfax, fourth son of William Fairfax, and the second by his second marriage, was educated at Wakefield school, in Yorkshire; served in the army, and was killed at the siege of Quebec. He was a young man of very promising abilities, and much esteemed by General Wolfe. When the general landed, he saw young Fairfax sitting upon the bank of the river, and immediately running up to him, he clapped him on the shoulder, and said, "Young man, when "we come to action, remember your name." Alas! they unfortunately both fell in the space of a few hours.

Hannah, youngest child of William Fairfax by his second

marriage, is married to Warner Washington, eldest son of General Washington's father's eldest brother, and the head of that now illustrious family. She has two sons and four daughters; all, except the youngest daughter, married to persons of condition and distinction in Virginia.

These anecdotes of the several branches of the Fairfax family, now domiciliated in Virginia, may, perhaps, not be unacceptable to the reader, and especially to the friends of that noble family. They are, I believe, correct, and may be relied upon. I received them from unquestionable authority, from a person intimately connected with the family; who, from repeated conversations with Thomas, late Lord Fairfax; Mr. William Fairfax; his son George William; Mrs. Mary Sherrard, first cousin to Thomas Lord Fairfax, and aunt to the present Earl of Harborough; Lady Lucy Sherrard; and many noble relatives of the family residing in the north of England; was well qualified to give the information.

DIARY

OF THE

WEATHER.

Fahrenheit's Thermometer.		JANUARY, 1760.					
		Days.	Hour Morn.	Ther.	Wind.	Weather.	Hour 2. After.
96	Vital heat.	1	8				
		2					
	Very	3					
85	hot.	4					
		5					
	Hot.	6					
75		7					
		8					
		9					
65	Warm air.	10					
		11					
		12					
		13					
55	Temper- ate.	14	—	10	N. W.	Quite clear.	
		15	....	10	N. W.	Clouded.	
		16	—	20	N. W.	Snow.	
	Cold	17	....	26	N. W.	Rain and freezing hard.	
45	air.	18	....	34	S. W.	A thaw.	
		19	....	36	S. W.	A thaw.	
		20	....	49	S. E.	Rain.	
	Frost.	21	—	36	N. E.	Rain.	
32		22	—	23	N. W.	Quite clear.	
		23	—	19	N. E.	Quite clear.	
		24	—	25	S. W.	Quite clear.	
	Hard	25	—	30	S. W.	Quite clear.	
20	frost.	26	....	25	S. E.	Quite clear.	
		27	—	40	S. W.	Rain.	
	Frost 1740.	28	—	24	S. W.	Quite clear.	
12		29	—	34	N. W.	Little cloudy.	
	Frost 1709.	30	—	34	S. W.	Cloudy.	
		31	—	24	N. W.	Quite clear.	

				FEBRUARY, 1760.	
DAYS.	HOUR Morn.	THER.	WIND.	WEATHER.	HOUR 2. After.
1	8	30	S. W.	Sleet and rain.	
2	——	26	S. E.	Quite clear.	
3	——	21	N. W.	Quite clear.	
4	——	31	S. E.	Quite clear.	
5	——	46	S.	Clouded.	
6	——	49	E.	Little clouded..........	62
7	——	46	S. W.	Quite clear	62
8	——	49	N. E.	Quite clear	58
9	——	33	E.	Quite clear.	
10	——	38	N. E.	Clouded	52
11	——	37	N.	Quite clear.	
12	——	28	S. W.	Quite clear.	
13	——	52	S. W.	Little clouded.........	66
14	——	56	S. W.	Hazy	70
15	——	38	N.	Misting rain.	
16	——	35	N.	Little cloudy.	
17	——	34	N. W.	Clouded, little snow.	
18	——	22	N. W.	Quite clear	30
19	——	25	S. W.	Quite clear	43
20	——	34	S. E.	Hazy.	48
21	——	41	S.	Hazy.	64
22	——	49	W.	Quite clear.	56
23	——	36	N. W.	Quite clear.	
24	——	40	S. W.	Little cloudy.	
25	——	45	S. E.	Quite clear.	56
26	——	53	S.	Hazy.	72
27	——	59	N. E.	Clouded	76
28	——	49	N. E.	Clouded	54
29	——	42	N. E.	Rain	37

				MARCH, 1760.	
DAYS.	HOUR Morn.	THER.	WIND.	WEATHER.	HOUR 2. After.
1	8	32	E.	Clouded.	
2		34	N.	Little cloudy.	
3		40	N. E.	Clouded	54
4		51	S. W.	Showery and windy	59
5		40	W.	Little cloudy and windy	45
6		35	S. W.	Quite clear	52
7		45	S. W.	Hazy.	54
8		48	S. W.	Rain	50
9		35	N.	Misting rain	38
10		32	W.	Clouded	45
11		32	N. E.	Little cloudy.	43
12		35	S. E.	Clouded.	54
13		49	S. E.	Rain	54
14		45	N. E.	Misting rain	43
15		37	N. E.	Clouded	39
16		30	N.	Thick snow .	32
17		26	N. W.	Snow	32
18		27	N. W.	Quite clear	38
19		39	S. W.	Clouded	52
20		41	N. W.	Cloudy	38
21		29	N. E.	Snow	34
22		36	N. E.	Rain	39
23		39	E.	Little cloudy	50
24		45	E.	Little cloudy	52
25		49	S. E.	Little cloudy	56
26		41	N. W.	Quite clear	48
27		43	S. W.	Quite clear	54
28		53	S. W.	Quite clear	70
29		64	S. W.	Hazy.	74
30		57	S. W.	Rain	67
31		66	W.	Showery	64

				APRIL, 1760.	
DAYS.	HOUR Morn.	THER.	WIND.	WEATHER.	HOUR 2. After.
I	8	49	N. W.	Quite clear	55
2		50	S.	Quite clear	67
3		61	S. W.	Clouded	70
4		65	S. E.	Quite clear	76
5		70	W.	Quite clear, thunder	79
6		57	E.	Clouded	60
7		50	N. W.	Thunder, clouded	65
8		47	N. E.	Thunder, clouded	50
9		45	N. E.	Clouded	50
10		64	S. W.	Little cloudy, thunder . .	85
11		44	N. E.	Small rain	52
12		53	N. E.	Little cloudy	56
13		53	S. E.	Clouded	69
14		67	S. W.	Little cloudy	73
15		70	S. W.	Cloudy, thunder	80
16		48	N. W.	Little cloudy	58
17		53	S. E.	Clouded	50
18		45	N. E.	Clouded	50
19		55	W.	Quite clear.	71
20		59	S. W.	Quite clear, thunder . . .	77
21		64	E.	Quite clear.	77
22		65	S. E.	Clouded	75
23		65	S. W.	Cloudy and showers	76
24		69	S. E.	Quite clear.	70
25		70	S. E.	Quite clear.	80
26		74	S. W.	Quite clear	84
27		77	S. W.	Quite clear, thunder	85
28		70	S. W.	Quite clear	80
29		65	N. W.	Quite clear	69
30		62	N. W.	Quite clear	60

			MAY, 1760.		

DAYS.	HOUR Morn.	THER.	WIND.	WEATHER.	HOUR 2. After.
1	8	50	N. W.	Quite clear	60
2	—	56	N. E.	Little cloudy	64
3	—	52	W.	Quite clear	64
4	—	64	S. W.	Quite clear	74
5	—	65	S. W.	Foggy, little rain	74
6	—	58	N. E.	Clouded	63
7	—	60	N. E.	Quite clear	69
8	—	60	S. E.	Quite clear	73
9	—	72	S. W.	Quite clear	81
10	—	71	S. W.	Quite clear, thunder	80
11	—	65	N. E.	Little cloudy	70
12	—	58	N. E.	Rain, thunder	57
13	—	60	S. W.	Cloudy, thunder	70
14	—	68	N. W.	Cloudy	70
15	—	67	W.	Little cloudy	72
16	—	73	S. W.	Clouded, little rain	77
17	—	78	S. W.	Little cloudy	83
18	—	74	W.	Cloudy, thunder	78
19	—	68	N. W.	Cloudy	75
20	—	66	N. W.	Little cloudy	75
21	—	72	N. E.	Quite clear	75
22	—	64	N. E.	Rain, thunder	61
23	—	58	N. E.	Clouded	69
24	—	73	W.	Rain, thunder	63
25	—	71	N. W.	Quite clear	78
26	—	76	—	Thunder	82
27	—	61		. . . .	68
28	—	64		. . . .	70
29	—	64		. . . .	70
30	—	69		. . . .	75
31	—	71		. . . .	75

				JUNE, 1760.	
DAYS.	HOUR MOTR.	THER.	WIND.	WEATHER.	HOUR 2. After.
1	8	77		. . . .	80
2		77		. . . .	83
3		80		. . . .	88
4		83		Thunder	88
5		62		Rain	70
6		65		Thunder	63
7		65		. . . .	73
8		67		. . . .	78
9		70		Rain	75
10		65		. . . .	75
11		74		. . . .	81
12		78		. . . .	89
13		80		. . . .	87
14		82		. . . .	89
15		86		. . . .	91
16		90		Thunder	90
17		78		Thunder	87
18		73		High wind	75
19		66		. . . .	75
20		78		. . . .	83
21		80		. . . .	89
22		73		. . . .	75
23		68		Rain, thunder	80
24		72		. . . .	78
25		76		. . . .	79
26		73		. . . .	80
27		76		Thunder.	80
28		80		. . . .	85
29		81		. . . .	83
30		75		. . . .	83

DAYS.	HOUR MORN.	THER.	WIND.	WEATHER.	HOUR 2. After.
			JULY, 1760.		
1	8	80	————	Thunder	86
2	—	75	————	. . . .	82
3	—	81	————	. . . .	89
4	—	87	————	Thunder	92
5	—	75	————	Rain	76
6	—	72	————	. . . .	78
7	—	72	————	. . . .	80
8	—	71	————	Small rain	78
9	—	73	————	Rain	83
10	—	75	————	. . . .	80
11	—	84	————	. . . .	86
12	—	84	————	. . . .	88
13	—	86	————	. . . .	92
14	—	87	————	. . . .	92
15	—	87	————	. . . .	91
16	—	83	————	Thunder.	83
17	—	77	————	Rain	81
18	—	75	————	Rain	84
19	—	80	————	Rain	83
20	—	77	————	Rain	78
21	—	75	————	. . . .	87
22	—	80	————	Thunder	88
23	—	84	————	Thunder	93
24	—	88	————	. . . .	93
25	—	89	————	Thunder	94
26	—	86	————	. . . .	88
27	—	78	————	. . . .	80
28	—	74	————	. . . .	77
29	—	80	————	. . . .	81
30	—	80	————	. . . .	82
31	—	72	————	Rain	78

AUGUST, 1760.

Days.	Hour Morn.	Ther.	Wind.	Weather.	Hour 2. After.
1	8	77		....	84
2	—	77			81
3	—	75		Rain	78
4	—	73		....	78
5	—	74		Rain	84
6	—	83		....	89
7	—	85		....	90
8	—	85			91
9	—	87		Thunder	92
10	—	87		....	91
11	—	89			93
12	—	89		Thunder	94
13	—	90		Thunder	94
14	—	80		Rain	86
15	—	84		Thunder	88
16	—	79		....	87
17	—	84		....	86
18	—	80		....	88
19	—	83		....	88
20	—	78		....	83
21	—	72		....	79
22	—	78		Rain	83
23	—	76		....	84
24	—	77		....	84
25	—	83		....	86
26	—	76		....	83
27	—	84		....	89
28	—	72		Thunder	78
29	—			....	
30	—	—		....	—
31	—	31		....	96

				SEPTEMBER, 1760.	
DAYS.	HOUR Morn.	THER.	WIND.	WEATHER.	HOUR 2. After.
1	8	85	....	Thunder	88
2	......	78	....	....	80
3	......	83	....	Thunder	88
4	......	80	....	....	82
5	......	70	....	....	76
6	......	73	....	....	78
7	......	73	....	....	78
8	......	75	....	....	81
9	......	80	....	....	86
10	......	80	....	A shower..........	87
11	......	80	....	....	86
12	......	80	....	....	83
13	......	76	....	....	78
14	......	69	....	....	80
15	......	82	....	A shower..........	91
16	......	71	....	....	72
17	......	67	....	Rain	72
18	......	55	....	....	62
19	......	64	....	....	68
20	......	52	....	....	65
21	......	49	....	....	64
22	......	63	....	....	76
23	......	71	....	....	79
24	......	62	....	....	70
25	......	52	....	....	64
26	......	52	....	....	69
27	......	58	....	....	71
28	......	64	....	....	77
29	......	59	....	Rain	67
30	......	58	....	....	67

				OCTOBER, *1760*.	
DAYS.	HOUR MORN.	THER.	WIND.	WEATHER.	HOUR 2. After.
1	8	54		. . . .	63
2		54		. . . .	67
3		55		. . . .	70
4		57		. . . .	73
5		58		. . . .	63
6		57		Misting rain	57
7		57		. . . .	59
8		58		. . . .	67
9		62		. . . .	68
10		62		. . . .	70
11		62		. . . .	70
12		50		. . . .	66
13		62		Rain	78
14		70		. . . .	68
15		49		. . . .	60
16		49		. . . .	59
17		45		Little rain	62
18		50		. . . .	68
19		54		. . . .	70
20		50		. . . .	53
21		48		. . . .	59
22		43		. . . .	57
23		42		Rain	60
24		63		. . . .	71
25		50		. . . .	58
26		48		. . . .	69
27		50		. . . .	63
28		45		Rain	60
29		45		. . . .	43
30		43		. . . .	49
31		30		. . . .	

Days.	Hour Morn.	Ther.	Wind.	Weather.	Hour 2. After.
NOVEMBER, 1760.					
1	8	43	——	. . . .	. . . .
2					
3					
4					
5	——	47	——	. . . .	61
6	——	50	——	. . . .	67
7	——	50	——	. . . .	70
8	——	54	——	. . . .	55
9	——	40	——	. . . .	48
10	——	35	——	. . . .	43
11	——	30	——	. . . .	45
12	——	43	——	. . . .	60
13	——	42	——	. . . .	52
14	——	40	——	. . . .	47
15	——	30	——	. . . .	46
16	——	42	——	. . . .	60
17	——	33	——	Little snow	37
18	——	25	——	. . . .	36
19	——	27	——	. . . .	38
20	——	35	——	. . . .	48
21	——	36	——	. . . .	47
22	——	28	——	. . . .	51
23	——	38	——	. . . .	58
24	——	48	——	. . . .	64
25	——	48	——	Little rain	54
26	——	49	——	Rain	60
27	——	51	——	Rain	55
28	——	41	——	. . . .	52
29	——	36	——	. . . .	45
30	——	33	——	. . . .	46

DAYS.	HOUR Morn.	THER.	WIND.	WEATHER.	HOUR 2. After.
			DECEMBER, 1760.		
1	8	30		. . . .	46
2		34		. . . .	49
3	....	41		Rain	47
4	———	51		. . . .	56
5	———	38		. . . .	47
6	———	35		. . . .	46
7	....	38		. . . .	48
8	....	35		. . . .	45
9	———	44		Rain	49
10	———	55		Rain	57
11	———	40		. . . .	55
12	———	44		. . . .	51
13	———	29		. . . .	46
14	———	32		. . . .	47
15	———	48		. . . .	65
16	———	63		Rain	69
17	———	27		. . . .	35
18	....	30		Snow	32
19	———	21		. . . .	34
20	———	24		Rain	38
21	———	44		Misting rain	55
22	———	32		. . . .	44
23					
24	....	25		. . . .	37
25	....	23		. . . .	38
26	———	32		. . . .	53
27	———	42		. . . .	54
28	———	42		Rain	—
29	———	44		. . . .	44
30	———	27		. . . .	35
31	....	24		. . . .	35

				JANUARY, 1761.	
Days.	Hour Morn.	Ther.	Wind.	Weather.	Hour 2. After.
1	8	29	N. W.	Clear	35
2	—	26	———	Snow	—
3	. . . . . .	27	N. W.	Flying clouds.	32
4	. . . .	10	N. W.	Clear	19
5	—	12	N. E.	Snow	29
6	——	22	N.	. . . .	28
7	——	20	N. E.	Snow	26
8	. . . . . .	23	N.	Clouded	33
9	—	23	S. W.	. . . .	41
10	——	27	N.	Clouded	32
11		21	N. W.	. . . .	32
12	. . . .	5	N.	Clouded	25
13	——	18	N. W.	. . . .	21
14	——	15	N.	Clouded	33
15	. . . .	28	N. W.	. . . .	44
16	——	36	W.	. . . .	41
17		28	N. E.		29
18	——	31	S. W.	Rain	44
19	——	34	W.	. . . .	44
20	——	28	S. W.	Flying clouds	54
21	. . . .	42	S. W.	Cloudy	54
22	——	32	N. W.	. . . .	34
23	——	22	N. W.	Cloudy	36
24	——	34	W.	Clouded	38
25	——	24	N. E.	Cloudy	32
26	——	35	S. W.	Cloudy	58
27	——	49	S.	Clouded	64
28	——	44	N. E.	. . . .	49
29	——	32	N. E.	Clouded	48
30	. . . . . .	46	S.	Clouded	62
31	—	46	N. W.	Flying clouds	48

DAYS.	HOUR MORN.	THER.	WIND.	WEATHER.	HOUR 2. AFER.
1	8	24	N. W.	. . . .	32
2	. . . . . .	34	S. W.	Cloudy	64
3	—	30	N. E.	Little snow	30
4	. . . . . .	22	N. W.	Flying clouds	26
5	—	15	N. W.	. . . .	24
6	. . . . . .	23	N. E.	Cloudy	36
7	—	45	S.	Clouded	60
8	—	57	S. W.	Cloudy	64
9	—	38	N. E.	Flying clouds	—
10	—	34	N. E.	Rain	37
11	. . . . . .	37	N. E.	Clouded	47
12	—	35	N. E.	Rain	40
13	. . . . . .	40	N. E.	Clouded	54
14	—	39	N. E.	Misting rain	42
15	—	38	N. E.	Rain	40
16	. . . . . .	37	N. E.	Rain	35
17	—	35	N. W.	. . . .	45
18	. . . . . .	35	S. E.	. . . .	60
19	—	36	S. W.	Flying clouds	59
20	. . . . . .	51	S. W.	Clouded	67
21	. . . . . .	49	W.	Flying clouds	57
22	. . . . . .	36	N. W.	Flying clouds	45
23	—	29	N.	. . . .	35
24	. . . . . .	22	N. W.	. . . .	35
25	. . . . . .	31	S. W.	. . . .	52
26	. . . . . .	49	S. W.	Hazy	67
27	. . . . . .	38	S. E.	Rain	40
28	—	35	N. W.	Sleet	40

FEBRUARY, 1761.

Days.	Hour Morn.	Ther.	Wind.	Weather.	Hour 2. After
				MARCH, 1761.	
1	8	28	N. W.	Flying clouds	37
2	—	28	N. E.	Clouded	43
3	—	32	W.	Snow	42
4	—	38	W.	....	48
5	—	42	S. W.	Clouded	56
6	—	33	N. W.	Clouded	38
7	—	31	N. E.	Snow	32
8	—	33	N. W.	Clouded	47
9	—	33	N. W.	....	43
10	—	36	S. W.	....	55
11	—	50	W.	Clouded	60
12	—	43	S. W.	Clouded	60
13	—	43	N. E.	Clouded	42
14	—	35	N.	Clouded	50
15	—	29	N. W.	....	38
16	—	35	S. W.	Clouded	58
17	—	43	N. E.	....	48
18	—	45	S. E.	Clouded	70
19	—	61	N. E.	Clouded	71
20	—	47	N. E.	Clouded	53
21	—	46	S. W.	Clouded	65
22	—	60	S.	Clouded	78
23	—	53	N.	....	57
24	—	45	N.	....	52
25	—	47	N. E.	....	56
26	—	54	S.	Hazy	74
27	—	63	S. W.	Hazy	83
28	—	62	S. W.	Hazy	82
29	—	68	S.	Hazy	86
30	—	61	S. W.	....	78
31	—	48	E.	Clouded	65

				APRIL, 1761.	
DAYS.	**HOUR Morn.**	**THER.**	**WIND.**	**WEATHER.**	**HOUR 2. After.**
1	8	58	N. E.	. . . .	70
2	---	55	S. E.	Hazy	69
3	---	61	S.	Cloudy	75
4	---	63	S.	Cloudy, thunder	73
5	---	50	N.	Rain	57
6	---	35	N. W.	. . . .	46
7	---	49	S. E.	Cloudy	66
8	---	57	S.	Clouded	69
9	---	60	E.	Rain	57
10	---	47	N. E.	Rain	50
11	---	47	S. E.	Rain	52
12	---	46	N. E.	Clouded	51
13	---	51	S. E.	Clouded	66
14	---	57	S.	Cloudy	77
15	---	69	S. W.	Flying clouds	83
16	---	74	S. W.	High wind	86
17	---	57	N. W.	. . . .	65
18	---	51	N. E.	. . . .	60
19	---	62	S. W.	. . . .	75
20	---	68	S. W.	Flying clouds	82
21	---	74	S. W.	Flying clouds	82
22	---	56	S. E.	Misting rain, thunder....	61
23	---	66	S. W.	Flying clouds	78
24	---	73	N.	Clouded	74
25	---	71	S. W.	Flying clouds	84
26	---	64	N. E.	. . . .	74
27	---	69	S.	Rain	---
28	---	70	S.	Little rain	86
29	---	---	---	. . . .	---
30	---	56	---	Little rain	50

				MAY, 1761.	
DAYS.	HOUR Morn.	THER.	WIND.	WEATHER.	HOUR 2. After.
1	8	58	——	Flying clouds	69
2	—	55	N. W.	....	64
3	—	58	N. E.	Rain	67
4	—	65	S.	Clouded, thunder	80
5	—	60	N. W.	....	69
6	—	57	N. E.	Flying clouds	63
7	—	52	N. E.	Clouded	54
8	—	53	E.	Rain	53
9	—	55	E.	High wind, rain	57
10	—	54	S. E.	Rain	64
11	—	60	S. E.	Rain	67
12	—	68	S.	Clouded	80
13	—	70	S. E.	Showery	73
14	—	60	N. E.	Showery	63
15	—	61	N. W.	Clouded	73
16	—	73	S. E.	Flying clouds	80
17	—	75	S.	Flying clouds	89
18	—	83	S. W.	Cloudy, thunder	87
19	—	67	N. W.	Flying clouds	76
20	—	60	N. W.	....	67
21					
22					
23					
24	—	80	S. W.	....	89
25					
26					
27					
28	—	54	——	Little rain	60
29	—	58	N. E.	Clouded	64
30	—	64	——	....	83
31	—	81	N. W.	Flying clouds	—

				JUNE, 1761.		
Days.	Hour Morn.	Ther.	Wind.	Weather.	Hour 2. After.
1	8	60	N. W.	. . . .	70
2	—	64	N. E.	Flying clouds	74
3	—	75	E.	Flying clouds	78
4	—	75	S.	Misting rain	—
5	—	64	N. W.	Flying clouds	71
6	—	64	N. E.	. . . .	72
7	—	70	S. E.	Flying clouds	76
8	—	68	E.	Clouded	72
9	—	68	E.	Little rain	72
10	—	73	N. E.	. . . .	76
11	—	75	E.	. . . .	76
12	—	77	S. E.	. . . .	82
13	—	79	S.	Clouded	86
14	—	85	S. W.	Flying clouds	87
15	—	85	S. W.	Flying clouds	87
16	—	85	N. E.	Flying clouds	87
17	—	88	N. E.	Flying clouds	88
18	—	86	S. W.	Flying clouds	88
19	—	86	S. W.	Clouded, thunder	91
20	—	60	N. E.	Rain	61
21	—	60	N. E.	Flying clouds	63
22	—	71	N. E.	Flying clouds	73
23	—	76	N.	. . . .	79
24	—	81	S.	. . . .	85
25	—	84	S. W.	Flying clouds	85
26	—	89	S. W.	Flying clouds	89
27	—	89	S. W.	. . . .	92
28	—	91	S.	. . . .	97
29	—	89	S. W.	. . . .	97
30	—	89	S. W.	Flying clouds, thunder . .	92

				JULY, 1761.	
DAYS.	HOUR MORN.	THER.	WIND.	WEATHER.	HOUR 2. After.
1	8	87	S. W.	Cloudy, thunder	92
2	—	90	S.	Flying clouds	94
3	—	91	S.	Flying clouds	93
4	—	92	S. W.	Flying clouds	94
5	—	93	S.	Clouded	94
6	—	95	S.	Clouded, thunder	97
7	—	87	S. W.	Flying clouds	94
8	—	92	S. W.	Flying clouds, thunder ..	88
9	—	89	S. W.	Showery	94
10	—	83	S. W.	Cloudy, thunder	92
11	—	62	N. E.	Small rain	66
12	—	70	E.	Flying clouds	76
13	—	79	S. E.	....	80
14	—	80	E.	....	80
15	—	84	S. W.	....	88
16	—	90	S.	Flying clouds	94
17	—	89	S. E.		86
18	—	94	S. W.	Flying clouds	92
19	—	91	S. W.	Flying clouds	95
20	—	91	S. W.	Flying clouds	94
21	—	93	S. W.	Cloudy, thunder	94
22	—	72	N. E.	Clouded	80
23	—	82	S. W.	Clear, thunder	93
24	—	80	N. E.	Clouded	81
25	—	72	N. E.	...... thunder	79
26	—	74	S. W.	Cloudy	86
27	—	86	S. W.	Cloudy	92
28	—	90	S. W.	Clouded	92
29	—	86	N. E.	Flying clouds	88
30	—	79	N. E.	....	86
31	—	—	S. W.	Flying clouds	90

				AUGUST, 1761.	
Days	Hour Morn.	Ther.	Wind.	Weather.	Hour 2. After.
1	8	88	S. W.	Cloudy, thunder	91
2	....	85	S. W.	Clouded, thunder	89
3	—	81	E.	Flying clouds	85
4	....	85	W.	Flying clouds	91
5	....			....	93
6					
7					
8					
9					
10					
11					
12					
13	....			....	97
14	......	85	S. W.	Flying clouds	93
15	—	86	S. W.	Flying clouds	93
16	—	90	S. W.	Flying clouds	94
17	....	89	S. W.	Flying clouds	94
18	....	88	S. W.	Cloudy	94
19	—	89	S. W.	Flying clouds, thunder ..	95
20	—	74	N. E.	Clouded	74
21	....	75	N. E.	Rain	76
22	....	66	N. E.	Clouded	77
23	—	64	N. W.	Rain	70
24	—	65	N.	Clouded	71
25	....	66	N.	Clouded	72
26	—	65	N.	Cloudy	74
27	—	69	N. W.	....	78
28	—	71	N. W.	....	81
29	—	78	W.	....	83
30	—	72	S. W.	Flying clouds	86
31	—	75	N. W.	Flying clouds	83

SEPTEMBER, 1761.					
DAYS.	HOUR Morn.	THER.	WIND.	WEATHER.	HOUR 2. After.
1	8	70	N. W.	Cloudy	78
2	———	69	N. E.	Rain	73
3	———	66	N. W.	Clouded	68
4	———	61	N. W.	Clouded	70
5	———	66	W.	....	73
6	———	71	S. W.	....	82
7	———	67	N.	Cloudy	74
8	———	64	N. W.	....	71
9	———	71	S. W.	Flying clouds	82
10	———	73	S. W.	Flying clouds, rain	83
11	———	62	N. W.	Cloudy	70
12	———	63	N. W.	....	73
13	———	64	N. W.	....	75
14	———	69	S. W.	....	80
15	———	65	N. E.	Clouded	74
16	———	62	N. E.	Cloudy	67
17	———	65	S. W.	Cloudy	77
18	———	66	N. W.	....	75
19	———	70	S. W.	....	81
20	———	70	S. E.	....	76
21	———	68	N. E.	Clouded	73
22	———	65	N. E.	Rain	78
23	———	75	S. E.	Rain	78
24	———	72	S. E.	Rain	87
25	———	81	S.	Cloudy	76
26	———	72	S.	Cloudy	85
27	———	74	S.	Clouded	84
28	———	76	S.	Flying clouds	82
29	———	72	S. E.	Flying clouds	80
30	———	74	S. E.	Cloudy	80

Appendix, N° 5

				OCTOBER, 1761.	
DAYS.	HOUR Morn.	THER.	WIND.	WEATHER.	HOUR 2. After.
1	8	70	N. E.	Small rain	71
2	——	67	N.	Small rain	70
3	——	67	N.	Cloudy	78
4	——	63	N.	Cloudy	71
5	——	65	N.	....	75
6	——	67	S. E..	....	76
7	——	70	S.	Cloudy	81
8	——	73	S.	Rain	83
9	——	63	N. E.	Rain	58
10	——	53	N. E.	Clouded	60
11	——	53	N. E.	Rain	52
12	——	51	N. E.	Cloudy	56
13	——	46	N. W.	....	56
14	——	46	N.	Flying clouds	57
15	——	47	N. W.	....	57
16	——	47	N.	....	60
17	——	53	W.	Flying clouds	68
18	——	55	S. W.	....	70
19	——	56	S. W.	....	72
20	——	58	S. E.	Cloudy	72
21	——	66	E.	Cloudy	71
22	——	67	S. E.	Rain	58
23	——	47	N. W.	Rain	46
24	——	45	S. W.	Flying clouds	58
25	——	45	W.	Clouded	58
26	——	45	N. W.	Clouded	58
27	——	50	N. W.	Clouded	57
28	——	45	N. W.	Flying clouds	51
29	——	43	N. E.	Cloudy	59
30	——	50	S. W.	Cloudy	59
31	——	51	S. W.	Flying clouds	65

				NOVEMBER, 1761.	
Days.	Hour Morn.	Ther.	Wind.	Weather.	Hour 2. After.
1	8	56	N. E.	Rain	51
2	—	43	N. W.	Flying clouds	55
3	—	43	N. W.	Flying clouds	59
4	—	50	S. E.	Rain	62
5	—	46	N. W.	Flying clouds	57
6	—	44	N. W.	Clouded	46
7	—	35	N. W.	....	46
8	—	30	N. W.	....	45
9	—	30	—	Clouded	—
10	—	35	—	Clouded	—
11	—	35	—	....	—
12	—	35	—	Flying clouds	52
13					
14	—	—	N. W.	....	47
15	—	35	N. W.	....	46
16	—	35	N. W.	....	51
17	—	40	N. W.	Rain	49
18	—	45	S. W.	....	56
19	—	41	S. W.	Small rain	42
20					
21	—	36	N. W.	....	49
22	—	35	N.	....	49
23	—	35	S. W.	....	54
24	—	34	N. E.	Foggy	50
25	—	50	S.	Rain	54
26	—	35	N. W.	Cloudy	43
27	—	29	N. W.	Rain	45
28	—	47	S.	Clouded	62
29	—	49	S. W.	....	61
30	—	43	N. E.	Cloudy	53

Appendix, N° 5

DECEMBER, 1761.					
Days.	Hour Morn.	Ther.	Wind.	Weather.	Hour 2. After.
1	8	41	N. W.	....	49
2	——	32	N. W.	Clouded	48
3	——	35	N.	Cloudy	45
4	——	36	E.	Rain	45
5	——	38	S.	Rain, high wind	52
6	——	30	N. W.	....	——
7	——	26	N. W.	....	34
8	——	21	N. W.	Little snow	34
9	——	34	W.	Rain and snow	34
10	——	20	N. W.	....	20
11	——	12	N. W.	....	32
12	——	34	S. W.	Clouded	47
13	——	34	N.	Rain	38
14	——	32	N. E.	Rain	38
15	——	34	N. E.	Clouded	37
16	——	22	N. W.	....	30
17	——	26	S. W.	Clouded	43
18	——	19	N. W.	....	25
19	——	20	N. E.	Little snow	30
20	——	26	S. W.	Clouded	——
21	——	30	N. W.	Clouded	39
22	——	36	S. W.	Cloudy	49
23	——	20	N. W.	....	30
24	——	27	N. W.	Snow, rain	41
25	——	37	S. W.	Flying clouds	——
26	——	10	N. W.	....	19
27	——	7	N. W.	....	19
28	——	15	N. W.	....	37
29	——	26	S. W.	Flying clouds	42
30	——	27	S. W.	....	45
31	——	30	S. W.	....	48

				JANUARY, 1762.	
DAYS.	HOUR Morn.	THER.	WIND.	WEATHER.	HOUR 2, After.
1	8	30	N.	. . . .	34
2	—	15	N. W.	. . . .	48
3	—	13	N. E.	Cloudy	42
4	—	30	N.	Thick fog	46
5	—	39	N. E.	Clouded	54
6	—	39	N. E.	Thick fog	53
7	—	45	N. E.	Thick fog	64
8	—	51	S.	Thick fog	65
9	—	50	S. W.	Clouded	56
10	—	30	N.	Snow	30
11	—	30	N.	. . . .	39
12	—	25	N.	. . . .	45
13	—	34	S. W.	Clouded	51
14	—	35	N.	. . . .	55
15	—	40	S. W.	. . . .	64
16					
17	—	50	N. E.	Misting rain	39
18	—	40	N. E.	Misting rain	45
19	—	40	N. E.	Misting rain	41
20	—	55	S. W.	Flying clouds	54
21	—	33	N. W.	Flying clouds	45
22	—	26	N. W.	Flying clouds	40
23	—	30	N. E.	Rain	41
24	—	36	W.	. . . .	43
25	—	20	N. W.	. . . .	29
26	—	19	N. W.	. . . .	37
27					
28					
29					
30					
31					

				FEBRUARY, 1762.	
DAYS	HOUR Morn.	THER.	WIND.	WEATHER.	HOUR 2. After
1	8	—	—	Clouded	40
2		28	N. W.	. . . .	40
3		33	S. W.	Cloudy	53
4	—	46	W.	Flying clouds	59
5		45	S.	Flying clouds, thunder . .	60
6		44	W.	. . . .	53
7	—	40	N. E.	Cloudy, thunder	50
8	—	39	N.	Cloudy	47
9		32	N. W.	Cloudy	42
10		35	N. E.	Snow, rain	36
11	—	32	N. W.	Clouded	42
12		32	N. W.	. . . .	42
13	—	31	N. W.	. . . .	48
14	—	31	N. E.	Cloudy	—
15	—	31	N. W.	. . . .	49
16		32	N. E.	Flying clouds	47
17		42	S. W.	Small rain	46
18	—	42	N. W.	. . . .	48
19		36	W.	Hazy	48
20		45	W.	Hazy	49
21	—	34	N. W.	. . . .	—
22		26	N. W.	. . . .	36
23		36	S. W.	Hazy	45
24	—	35	N. W.	Clouded	45
25		23	N. W.	. . . .	26
26		24	N. W.	Flying clouds	30
27	—	22	N. W.	. . . .	32
28	—	30	N. W.	. . . .	31

				MARCH, 1762.	
DAYS.	**HOUR Morn.**	**THER.**	**WIND.**	**WEATHER.**	**HOUR 2. After**
1	8	28	N. W.	Hazy, rain	47
2	—	34	N. W.	Clouded	40
3	—	26	N. W.	....	40
4	—	36	W.	Flying clouds	51
5	—	32	N. E.	....	43
6	—	35	N. E.	Flying clouds	40
7	—	39	E.	Rain	43
8	—	37	N. E.	Rain	41
9	—	33	N. W.	....	—
10	—	33	N. W.	....	43
11	—	37	W.	....	49
12	—	41	S. E.	Rain	46
13	—	35	———	Cloudy	43
14	—	32	N. W.	Little snow	36
15	—	29	N. W.	....	36
16	—	34	N.	Cloudy	45
17	—	39	S. W.	Small rain	59
18	—	56	S. W.	Flying clouds	66
19	—	34	N. E.	Rain	43
20	—	43	S. E.	....	49
21	—	47	S.	Small rain	56
22	—	42	N. W.	....	51
23	—	35	N. E.	Cloudy	42
24	—	44	S. E.	Cloudy	53
25	—	41	N. E.	....	47
26	—	38	N. E.	....	48
27	—	44	S.	Hazy	58
28	—	53	S.	Clouded	59
29	—	58	S. W.	Flying clouds	65
30	—	44	N. E.	Cloudy	55
31	—	41	N. E.	Rain	45

Appendix, N° 5

				APRIL, 1762.	
DAYS.	HOUR Morn.	THER.	WIND.	WEATHER.	HOUR 2. After.
1	8	44	S. E.	Flying clouds	50
2	----	43	N. E.	Rain	46
3	----	52	S.	Cloudy	63
4	----	44	N. E.	. . . .	50
5	----	46	S. E.	Clouded	53
6	----	61	S.	. . . .	----
7	----	45	S. E.	Clouded	47
8	----	46	S. E.	Cloudy	57
9	----	45	N. W.	. . . .	51
10	----	49	N. W.	. . . .	58
11	----	52	S. W.	Hazy	70
12	----	61	S. W.	Hazy	73
13	----	63	S. W.	Hazy	73
14	----	45	N. E.	Rain	43
15	----	45	N. E.	Cloudy	50
16	----	50	S. W.	Clouded	64
17	----	50	N. W.	. . . .	59
18	----	50	S. W.	. . . .	65
19	----	56	N.	. . . .	60
20	----	42	N. E.	Rain	52
21	----	42	N. W.	. . . .	51
22	----	50	N. W.	. . . .	55
23	----	56	S. E.	. . . .	60
24	----	56	S. E.	. . . .	60
25	----	63	S.	. . . .	74
26	----	68	S. W.	Clouded	72
27	----	63	N.	. . . .	67
28	----	60	N. E.	Cloudy	64
29	----	56	S. W.	Hazy	73
30	----	71	S. W.	Hazy, thunder	81

MAY, 1762.

DAYS.	HOUR Morn.	THER.	WIND.	WEATHER.	HOUR 2. After.
1	8	72	S.W.	Showers	75
2	—	58	N. E.	Showers	55
3	—	53	N. E.	Rain	50
4	—	53	N. E.	Cloudy	58
5	—	56	S. W.	....	67
6	—	57	S. W.	Cloudy, thunder	65
7	—	56	N.	Flying clouds	61
8	—	59	E.	....	64
9	—	64	S.	....	69
10	—	63	N. E.	Cloudy	64
11	—	56		....	—
12	—	59	S.	Flying clouds	69
13	—	69	S. W.	Cloudy	79
14	—	56	N. E.	Clouded	55
15	—	56	E.	Cloudy	60
16	—	66	S. W.	Cloudy	72
17	—	70	S. W.	Thunder	79
18	—	74	S. W.	....	79
19	—	75	S. W.	....	79
20	—	76	S. W.	....	81
21	—	78	S.	Flying clouds	76
22	—	75	E.	Cloudy	73
23	—	77	S. W.	....	80
24	—	76	S. W.	....	81
25	—	80	S. W.	....	83
26	—	78	W.	....	84
27	—	80	S. W.	Flying clouds, thunder ..	82
28	—	65	N. W.	Rain	58
29	—	65	N.	Cloudy	71
30	—	69	N. E.	Cloudy	71
31	—	71	S. E.	Cloudy	75

				JUNE, 1762.	
Days.	Hour Morn.	Ther.	Wind.	Weather.	Hour 2. After.
I	8	71	S. W.	Clouded	74
2	—	67	N. W.	Cloudy	78
3	—	57	N. W.	Cloudy	60
4	—	60	N. W.	Flying clouds	66
5	—	—	—	....	73
6	—	75	S. W.	....	78
7	—	75	S. W.	....	82
8	—	77	S. E.	....	82
9	—	72	S. W.	....	82
10	—	78	S. W.	Cloudy, thunder	84
11	—	70	N.	....	75
12	—	79	S. E.	Flying clouds	79
13	—	70	S.	Cloudy	85
14	—	81	S.	Flying clouds, thunder ..	85
15	—	78	N. W.	Cloudy	82
16	—	83	N.	Cloudy, thunder	88
17	—	73	N. E.	Cloudy, thunder	80
18	—	74	N. W.	Rain	83
19	—	68	N. E.	Flying clouds	70
20	—	70	W.	Flying clouds	75
21	—	82	W.	....	80
22	—	87	W.	...... a shower	90
23	—	83	N. W.	Cloudy	79
24	—	73	E.	Cloudy	75
25	—	79	S. E.	Flying clouds	82
26	—	82	S. E.	....	75
27	—	84	S.	....	85
28	—	75	N. E.	....	83
29	—	82	S. E.	Flying clouds, thunder ..	87
30	—	70	N.	Clouded	79

				JULY, 1762.	

DAYS.	HOUR Morn.	THER.	WIND.	WEATHER.	HOUR 2. After.
1	8	73	E.	Rain	79
2	—	64	N. E.	Rain	70
3	—	66	W.	. . . .	79
4	. . . .	84	S. W.	. . . .	84
5	—	84	S. W.	Hazy	86
6	—	88	S. W.	Hazy, thunder	91
7	—	84	W.	Hazy, thunder	88
8	—	84	S. W.	Cloudy, thunder	88
9	—	76	N. E.	Flying clouds	76
10	—	73	N. E.	Flying clouds	73
11	—	79	S. E.	. . . .	80
12	—	75	S. W.	Clouded, a shower	82
13	—	80	S. W.	Clouded	84
14	—	80	S. E.	Cloudy	79
15	—	75	N.W.	Flying clouds	77
16	—	75	N. E.	Cloudy	80
17	—	83	S. E.	Flying clouds	82
18	—	82	S. W.	Flying clouds	84
19	—	83	S. W.	Flying clouds, thunder . . .	85
20	—	83	S. W.	Flying clouds	84
21	—	81	S. W.	Flying clouds	85
22	—	76	N. E.	Cloudy, thunder	85
23	—	85	S. E.	Cloudy	89
24	—	85	S.W.	Flying clouds	87
25	—	80	N.	Flying clouds	85
26	—	80	N. E.	Flying clouds	80
27	—	79	E.	Cloudy	79
28	—	81	S. E.	Flying clouds	79
29	—	81	S.	Flying clouds	85
30	—	84	E.	Cloudy	79
31	—	64	N. E.	Rain	62

Appendix, N° 5

				AUGUST, 1762.	
Days.	Hour Morn.	Ther.	Wind.	Weather.	Hour 2. After.
1	8	59	N. E.	Rain	62
2		70	N. W.	Flying clouds	76
3	—	67	N. E.	Flying clouds	70
4	—	67	N. E.	Flying clouds	69
5	—	66	N.	. . . .	74
6	—	67	W .	. . . .	74
7	—	74	S. W.	Flying clouds	79
8	—	74	S. W.	Flying clouds	79
9	—	72	S. W.	Flying clouds	2
10	—	69	N. W.	. . . .	75
11	—	71	S. W.	Cloudy	80
12	—	79	N.	Cloudy	84
13	—	73	N. E.	Cloudy	79
14	—	79	S. W.	Cloudy	84
15	—	78	S.	Flying clouds	84
16	—	78	S. W.	Clouded, thunder	82
17	—	77	S. W.	Flying clouds, shower . .	84
18	—	79	S. W.	Cloudy, thunder	83
19	—	80	S. W.	Cloudy, thunder	83
20	—	77	S. W.	Cloudy, thunder	84
21	—	67	N. W.	Cloudy	81
22	—	78	S. W.	Flying clouds	81
23	—	78	S. W.	Cloudy	83
24	—	78	S. W.	Flying clouds, thunder . .	83
25	—	69	N. W.	Cloudy, thunder	75
26	—	73	N. E.	Cloudy, thunder	80
27	—	74	S. W.	Cloudy	82
28	—	76	S. W.	Cloudy	83
29	—	76	S. W.	Flying clouds	83
30	—	77	S. W.	Flying clouds	82
31	—	73	N. W.	Flying clouds	81

				SEPTEMBER, 1762.	
DAYS.	HOUR Morn.	THER.	WIND.	WEATHER.	HOUR 2. After.
1	8	71	N.	Cloudy	78
2	------	77	N.	Cloudy	75
3	------	64	N. E.	Cloudy	68
4	------	65	N. E.	Flying clouds	69
5	------	63	S.	Flying clouds	—
6	------	71	S. W.	Rain	81
7	------	61	N. E.	Cloudy	68
8	------	62	N. W.	....	68
9	------	64	N. E.	....	72
10	------	64	S. W.	....	76
11	------	72	N. E.	Cloudy	80
12	------	65	N. W.	Cloudy	74
13	------	67	N. E.	....	77
14	------	72	S. W.	...... thunder	82
15	------	69	N.	Flying clouds	77
16	------	67	N. W.	Flying clouds	74
17	------	59	N. E.	....	64
18	------	60	E.	Cloudy	80
19	------	64	S.	Cloudy	77
20	------	69	N. E.	Cloudy	81
21	------	70	W.	Cloudy, thunder	81
22	------	70	S. W.	Small rain	57
23	------	55	N. W.	....	59
24	------	51	N. W.	....	62
25	------	51	N.	Cloudy	64
26	------	55	N. E.	Cloudy	72
27	------	56	E.	Cloudy	73
28	------	64	S.	Rain	70
29	------	63	S.	Flying clouds	67
30	------	56	N. W.	....	67

				OCTOBER, *1762.*	
Days.	Hour Morn.	Ther.	Wind.	Weather.	Hour 2. After.
1	8	60	N.	. . . .	65
2	—	50	N. E.	. . . .	59
3	—	56	S. W.	. . . .	67
4	—	65	S. W.	Cloudy	74
5	—	60	W.	Rain	65
6	—	53	N. W.	Flying clouds	61
7	—	58	S. E.	Flying clouds	63
8	—	61	S.	Clouded	75
9	—	59	N. E.	Rain	61
10	—	63	S. W.	Clouded	71
11	—	59	N. E.	Cloudy	64
12	—	47	S. W.	. . . .	55
13	—	49	N.	Flying clouds	59
14	—	51	N. E.	Rain	58
15	—	60	S. W.	Rain	58
16	—	52	N. W.	Clouded	57
17	—	52	S. W.	Cloudy, thunder and hail .	65
18	—	51	N. W.	Cloudy	58
19	—	45	N. W.	Clouded	60
20	—	52	W.	Rain, thunder	56
21	—	43	N. W.	Cloudy	51
22	—	40	W.	. . . .	51
23	—	39	W.	. . . . thunder	54
24	—	49	S. W.	Rain	60
25	—	44	W.	Flying clouds	64
26	—	44	S.	Little rain	52
27	—	36	N. W.	Clouded	46
28	—	33	N. W.	Little snow	45
29	—	32	N. W.	. . . .	45
30	—	44	S. W.	. . . .	—
31	—	46	N. E.	Cloudy	53

				NOVEMBER, 1762.	
DAYS	HOUR Morn.	THER.	WIND.	WEATHER.	HOUR 2. After.
1	8	44	S. E.	Cloudy	58
2	----	50	S.	Flying clouds	66
3	----	53	N. W.	. . . .	61
4	----	42	N. W.	Flying clouds	65
5	----	51	S. E.	Rain	43
6	----	36	N. E.	Rain	34
7	----	34	N. E.	Clouded	----
8	----	32	N. W.	Cloudy	41
9	----	40	W.	Cloudy	46
10	----	35	N. E.	Clouded	44
11	----	38	N. W.	Cloudy	47
12	----	39	W.	Clouded	48
13	----	36	N. W.	Cloudy	45
14	----	31	N. W.	. . . .	42
15	----	31	N. W.	Flying clouds	48
16	----	41	S W.	. . . .	48
17	----	34	N. W.	. . . .	42
18	----	31	N. W.	. . . .	44
19	----	42	----	Foggy	----
20	----	41	N. W.	. . . .	47
21	----	42	N. E.	. . . .	45
22	----	35	N. E.	. . . .	58
23	----	45	N. E.	Foggy	60
24	----	46	N. E.	Foggy	52
25	----	44	S. E.	Foggy	52
26	----	48	N.	Foggy	49
27	----	38	E.	Clouded	46
28	----	40	N. E.	Rain	46
29	----	41	E.	Misting rain	47
30	----	43	W.	Flying clouds	48

DAYS.	HOUR Morn.	THER.	WIND.	WEATHER.	HOUR 2. After.
				DECEMBER, *1762*.	
1	8	31	N. W.	....	44
2	......	33	N.	....	45
3	......	43	S. W.	Clouded	46
4	......	44	S. W.	Hazy	56
5	......	43	S. W.	Hazy	45
6	......	36	N. W.	Clouded	44
7	......	37	S. W.	Small rain	42
8	......	33	N. W.	Clouded	42
9	......	32	N. W.	....	47
10	......	34	W.	Cloudy	52
11	......	35	S. W.	....	56
12	......	52	S.	Clouded	62
13	......	44	S. W.	Flying clouds	55
14	......	40	N. W.	Clouded	41
15	......	30	N. W.	Clouded	36
16	......	24	N. W.	....	41
17	......	30	N. W.	Cloudy	49
18	......	51	S. W.	Clouded	44
19	......	42	N. E.	Rain	43
20	......	40	N.	Misting rain	42
21	......	40	W.	Clouded	47
22	......	50	S. W.	Cloudy	59
23	......	41	N. E.	Rain	41
24	......	40	N. E.	Rain	41
25	......	41	N. E.	Rain	43
26	......	31	N. W.	....	35
27	......	26	N. W.	....	34
28	......	28	N. W.	....	41
29	......	30	N. E.	Foggy	46
30	......	44	N. E.	Misting rain	50
31	......	44	S. W.	Foggy	48

EDITORIAL NOTES.

NOTE I.

THE present-day visitor to Williamsburg finds it one of the most charmingly antique towns in America. Duke of Gloucester, the main street of the village, broadens at its centre into an open square called Court House Green, where stands an ancient temple of justice, surrounded by fine colonial residences. Farther up Duke of Gloucester Street is another square, Palace Green, faced by other historic mansions, including the old palace of the royal governors. Thence a short walk takes one to the ancient church of Bruton parish, the oldest Protestant house of worship still in use in America; and at the end of the street stands the restored William and Mary College. The site of the old hall of the House of Burgesses is at the other end of Duke of Gloucester Street, but nothing remains of this famous structure save the foundation, and masses of broken plaster from its walls.

NOTE II.

The region beyond the Ohio, now the States of Ohio, Indiana and Illinois, was a part of the province of Virginia under her charter, but in 1781 was ceded to the Federal

Notes

Government. See Hinsdale's "The Old Northwest, with a View of the Thirteen Colonies as Constituted by the Royal Charters," New York, 1899.

NOTE III.

Colonel William Byrd, of Westover, founder of the towns of Richmond and Petersburg, was one of the most brilliant figures in the history of the later colonial period. Born to an ample fortune, the epitaph above his grave at Westover records that he "was sent early to England, where he made a happy proficiency in polite and various learning; contracted a most intimate and bosom friendship with the learned and illustrious Charles Boyle, Earl of Orrery; was called to the bar of the Middle Temple; was chosen Fellow of the Royal Society, and being thirty-seven years a member, at last became president of the council of this colony." His epitaph also tells the wayfarer that he was "the well-bred gentleman and polite companion, the constant enemy of all exorbitant power, and hearty friend of the liberties of his country." The famous "Westover Manuscripts," written by Byrd for his own amusement and first published in 1841, is one of the most delightful books that has come down to us from the colonial period.

NOTE IV.

Henry Bouquet, born in Rolle, Switzerland, in 1719, served in the armies of Holland and Sardinia, and in 1756 entered the British service with the rank of lieutenant-colonel. He took part in the expedition against Fort Duquesne in 1758 and was present at its capture. Five years later he successfully led an expedition to the relief of the same fort, then called Fort Pitt. In October, 1764, he marched against the Ohio Indians, who were harrying the border, and compelled the Shawnees, Delawares and other tribes to make peace at Tuscarawas. He was made colonel in 1762, and at the time of his death, which occurred at Pensacola in 1766, held the rank of brigadier-general. An account of Bouquet's expedition against the Ohio Indians, written by Dr. William Smith, then provost of the College of Philadelphia, and published in 1766, was reprinted at Cincinnati in 1868 with preface by Francis Parkman.

NOTE V.

Spotswood's iron works were located near the present Germanna Ford on the Rapidan. There is an engaging account of a visit to them in the "Westover Manuscripts."

NOTE VI.

The parsons were right both in law and in equity, but popular greed and prejudice were against them. It was as counsel for the defence in one of the suits growing out of this affair that, in 1763, Patrick Henry, then a young lawyer of twenty-seven, first proved his supreme powers as an orator, and at the same time startled his auditors with the bold declaration "that a king, by disallowing acts of a salutary nature, from being the father of his people, degenerated into a tyrant, and forfeited all right to his subjects' obedience." A full and satisfying account of the Parsons' Cause will be found in the first volume of William Wirt Henry's "Patrick Henry: Life, Correspondence and Speeches," New York, 1891.

Notes

NOTE VII.

George Wythe, described by Thomas Jefferson as "the Cato of his country without the avarice of the Roman," was born in 1726, and was early chosen a member of the House of Burgesses where he served until the opening of the Revolution. A leader from the first in the Patriot cause, he was, in August, 1775, appointed a delegate to the Continental Congress from Virginia, and as such signed the Declaration of Independence. He became speaker of the Virginia House of Delegates in 1777, and a little later was made chancellor of the State, which post he held for more than twenty years. For ten years following 1779 he was also professor of law in William and Mary College, and in 1787 served as a member of the convention that framed the Federal Constitution. His death in his eighty-first year was due to poison, administered, it was believed, by his nephew, who was tried for the crime but acquitted

NOTE VIII.

David Douglas was from 1758 to 1774 manager of the American Company, the most important organization of players in the colonies. He also built the first permanent theatres in New York, Philadelphia and Charleston. At the opening of the Revolution he withdrew to Jamaica, where, following his retirement, he held the posts of master in chancery and magistrate. He died in 1786

NOTE IX.

James Logan, born in Ireland in 1674, was from 1699 until his death in 1751 the business agent in Pennsylvania of William Penn and his heirs, and, Benjamin Franklin excepted, the ablest and most influential citizen of that province, serving at different times as member and president of the provincial council, justice of the court of common pleas, mayor of Philadelphia, chief justice and governor. His library of 2,000 volumes which he bequeathed to the city of Philadelphia was in 1792 annexed to the Philadelphia Library, established in 1731 by Franklin and now housed at the corner of Locust and Juniper streets in that city, but has been kept separate under the name of the Loganian Library.

Note X.

St. George's Chapel stood at the corner of the present Beekman and Cliff Streets, New York. Built and opened in 1752, it was rebuilt after its destruction by fire in 1814, and was occupied until 1841, when it was demolished and its congregation removed to the present church in Rutherford Place. Warehouses now cover its site and the burial ground which aforetime surrounded it.

Note XI.

The prison referred to by Burnaby stood in City Hall Park, New York, on the line of the present Park Row. Built in 1756, it was originally a graystone structure surmounted by a tower which was long a famous outlook for fires. During the Revolution and the British occupation of New York it was used as a Patriot prison. Then it became a place of detention for delinquent debtors, and served that purpose until 1829, when the common council decided to reconstruct it and devote it to the housing of the city records It was accordingly cut down a story

Notes

and encased in new outer walls, and as the Hall of Records remained one of the historic landmarks of the city until 1903, when it was torn down because it obstructed the route of the underground railway.

NOTE XII.

The fort of Burnaby's time was the successor of the one built by the Dutch founders of New York. It stood just south of Bowling Green, but was demolished in 1790 to furnish a site, first for an official residence for the governors of the State, then for a row of dwellings, and finally for a custom-house.

NOTE XIII.

The history of New York's first public library is an interesting one. In 1729 a collection of books bequeathed by John Millington, rector of Newington, England, to the Society for the Propagation of the Gospel in Foreign Parts, was by that organization presented to the city for a public library. At the same time like disposition was made of a collection presented to the society in 1700 by the Reverend John Sharp, chaplain of Lord Bellomont, then royal governor of New York. A quarter of a century later a number of citizens organized themselves into a body, which in due time received a royal charter under the name of the New York Society Library. Its collection of books housed in the old city hall in Wall Street grew steadily until the Revolution, during which it was scattered and almost totally destroyed by the British soldiery. The society reorganized, however, in 1783, and reviving its charter again began the collection of books. A building was erected in Nassau Street in 1793, but the

collection soon outgrew its quarters, and removing to
Chambers Street the society continued there until 1840
when it occupied a building of its own at the corner of
Broadway and Leonard Street. Hardly was it settled
here when the growth of the business section of the city
forced it to seek new quarters. It established itself for
a time in Astor Place, and then in 1857 removed to its
present home in University Place.

NOTE XIV.

Money for the founding of what in Burnaby's time was
King's College and is now Columbia University was raised
by a public lottery set afoot by the provincial assembly of
New York. Trinity Church gave it for a site the plot of
ground now bounded by College Place, and by Church,
Murray and Barclay Streets; and the three-story building
of stone erected thereon was first occupied in 1760, six
years after the college received its charter. Samuel Johnson, who forty years before had helped in the founding of
Yale College, was its first president, and had at the outset
but a single assistant. The first graduating class, that of
1758, numbered only eight; but the college grew from
year to year in numbers and efficiency, and when Dr.
Johnson resigned the presidency, in 1763, he had laid a
sure foundation for his successors.

NOTE XV.

Two Kissing Bridges have a place in the early history
of New York. In the opening years of the last century, a
small stream called the Saw-kill was spanned at the present
intersection of Third Avenue and Seventy-seventh Street

Notes

by a bridge which John Randel, Jr., declares was known to all the young men and women of his day as the Kissing Bridge. The Kissing Bridge of Burnaby's time, however, spanned a creek in what is now the Bowery, a little to the south of the present Chatham Square

NOTE XVI.

The Redwood Library, chartered in 1747, takes its name from Abraham Redwood (1709-1788), a benevolent Quaker merchant of Newport, who was one of its founders. The building in which it is housed, a handsome Doric structure completed in 1750, was designed by Peter Harrison, the architect of Blenheim Castle.

NOTE XVII.

In 1725, the famous George Berkeley, then dean of Derry, conceived the idea of converting the American Indians to Christianity by means of a college to be established in the Bermuda Islands. Sir Robert Walpole, at that time chief minister, opposed the enterprise, but Berkeley persuaded the British government to promise a grant of £20,000 in support of his plans, and in September, 1728, he sailed for America, expecting to found the college and assume its presidency. He reached Newport in January, 1729, where he bought a farm, erected upon it a small house, engaged in correspondence and study, composed "The Minute Philosopher," preached occasionally, and waited in vain for the expected endowment. Finally, wearied by long delays and reluctantly convinced that Walpole had no intention of giving him the promised support, Berkeley gave up his residence at Newport, and, after a short stay in Boston, in September, 1731, set sail for home. Three years after his return to England he became bishop of Cloyne. He died in 1753 at the age of sixty-nine.

NOTE XVIII.

John Smibert, who was to have been professor of fine arts in Berkeley's projected college, was born in Edinburgh in 1684, studied painting in London, and then passed some years in Italy. Returning to England he became a portrait painter in London, and, in 1729, came to America with Berkeley. He painted for some months in Newport, and when the Bermuda enterprise was abandoned settled in Boston. When Berkeley became bishop of Cloyne, he asked Smibert to join him in Ireland, but the painter, who in the meantime had married a wealthy widow, declined his patron's invitation, and dwelt in Boston, prosperous and contented until his death in 1751. Smibert's most important American work is the painting of Berkeley and his family, executed in Boston in the summer of 1731, and presented to Yale College in 1808.

NOTE XIX.

A native of Sussex, England, and born in 1693, William Shirley at the age of forty-one settled in Boston in the practice of his profession — the law. He served as governor of Massachusetts from 1741 to 1745, and in the latter year planned the successful expedition against Cape Breton. He was in England from 1745 to 1753, but then returned to Massachusetts as governor, and at the opening of the French war in 1755 was commander-in-chief of the British forces in North America. He was made lieutenant-general in 1759, and later served as governor of the Bahama Islands. He returned to Massachusetts in 1770, and died in the following year at Roxbury.

NOTE XX.

Under the name of "bundling" the custom described by Burnaby prevailed until a recent period in the sections of Pennsylvania originally settled by Germans. The curious will find the subject exhaustively treated in Henry Reed Stiles' "Bundling: its origin, progress and decline in America," Albany, 1871.

INDEX

Index

Index